THAT BODY IMAGE THING

Young Women Speak Out

Edited by Sara Torres
October 1999

CRIAW/ICREF acknowledges the financial assistance of the Women's Program, Status of Women Canada, in the production of this publication.

The ideas expressed in this document are those of the authors and do not necessarily reflect those of CRIAW or the Women's Program, Status of Women Canada.

EDITING TEAM

Vijay Agnew
Céline Bessette
Susannah Bush (resource section)
Barbara Cottrell
Lise Martin
Marika Morris
Martha Muzychka

Sara Torres (Project Coordinator)

PUBLICATIONS COMMITTEE MEMBERS

Vijay Agnew
Micheline Beauregard - (francophone editor Québec)
Karen Blackford
Elsy Gagné
Marylea MacDonald
Ellen O'Reilly
Carmen Poulin - (francophone editor outside Québec)
Eliane L. Silverman
Anne Tayler (anglophone editor)
Sara Torres (staff liaison)

Cover Design & Desktop publishing - TUTTI FRUTTI

Cover Design Photo by Joanne Rycaj Guillemette

© CRIAW

Published October 1999
by CRIAW/ICREF
    151 Slater Street, Suite 408
    Ottawa, ON
    K1P 5H3

ISBN 0-919653-83-9

Acknowledgements

This book would not have been possible without the participation of the young women who took the initiative and wrote personal essays for the competition "It is your body, write on it." We thank them for sharing their struggles, hopes, joys and sorrows with us. We also thank *Chatelaine* Magazine for co-sponsoring the writing contest with us.

We are indebted to the teachers and parents who encouraged the women to write about their experiences of their changing bodies and identities. We thank the young women of the Canterbury School of Art and the Ottawa University Arts Program who shared their drawings and photos illustrating the relationship between body and art. The Girls of the Gender Issues Group of the Vincent Massey Collegiate in Winnipeg, the Big Sisters Program of Ottawa-Carleton and the young women from the Canterbury School of Art participated in focus groups, discussions, and consultations and we are grateful to them as well for guiding us in the design and marketing of this book.

Many CRIAW board members, staff and other individuals contributed their expertise, advice and skills to making this book possible: Vijay Agnew, Micheline Beauregard, Natalie Beausoleil, Céline Bessette, Catherine Boldt, Susannah Bush, Hilary Burke, Marjolaine Côté, Barbara Cottrell, Tim Desclouds, Elsy Gagné, Anna Humphrey, Gayle Kells, Lise Martin, Chairmaine McCraw, Martha Muzchyka, Sherri Moore-Arbour, Marika Morris, Carmen Poulin, Anne Tayler, Danielle Trepanier, Michelle Wardman and *Chatelaine* Health Editor Amy Cross.

CRIAW Communications Officer Sara Torres coordinated the publication of this project from beginning to end, consulting with advisory committee members across the country, working with *Chatelaine* magazine, organizing focus groups, putting together the various aspects of the book, dealing with designers and printers, and ensuring every last detail was in place. CRIAW Executive Director Lise Martin contributed not only her experience and skills, but also her calm presence and support at every stage. Thank you!

Canadian Research Institute for the Advancement of Women

Contents

Acknowledgements — 3

Preface — 7
CRIAW President Catherine Boldt

Introduction — 9
Vijay Agnew

Part One: Voices of young women 16 to 19 — 11

Self-portrait of an Eighteen Year Old Girl-Inside\out by Anna Humphrey	13
Around the Next Corner by Kat Aubrey	15
El Cuerpo Es Mio (My Body Is Mine) by Emily Bodenberg	17
No Title by Alison Browne	20
The Sculpture by Gillian Burrell	23
A Short History of a Body by Amelia DeFalco	25
Girl Power by Laura Farina	29
Figuratively Speaking by Denise Fuller	31
No Title by Cheryl Amanda Gullage	34
No Title by Chellby	36
Me And My Body (and of course, my body hair) by Alice Honan	40
A Resting Place For Pink Daisies? by S. D. James	42
The Invisible Corset by Sarah Jasper	46
No Title by Candice Jwaszko	48
Body Image by Madiha Khan	50
No Title by Emily Lam	55
The Most Incredible Thing I Ever Did With My Body by Jennifer Mills	57
On The Lake by Larissa Mornryk	59
The Low Road by K. A. P.	61

Contents

A Little Bit Tired by Amy Lynn Rand	63
Seeing Past The Mirror And Beyond My Body by Rebecca Silver-Slayter	67
The Dance to Freedom by Pandora Syperek	71
No Title by Jessica Wilford	73

PART TWO: Voices of young women 13 to 15 — 75

The Dance by Charmaine McCraw	77
Deadly Battles by Becca Digout	79
"Dying to be Free" by Erin Dowling	82
My Struggle and Glory by Yenny Espinal	86
No Title by Lindsay Friis	88
Late Developer by Alison Louder	91
The Ultimate Connection by Jennifer MacDonald	93
It's My Body by Ashley Portielje	96
Armadillo by Emma Ziolkowska	98

CONCLUSION — 101
Marika Morris

AFTERWORD — 105
Natalie Beausoleil

RESOURCES — 111
Susannah Bush

Preface

When I first suggested a national body image essay contest for young women, I envisioned a book of insightful personal essays with a resource list for young women and those who care about them. I am proud this two year project has finally become the book you now hold in your hands. It would not have been possible without the hard work of the CRIAW staff, our advisory committees, and the support and participation of *Chatelaine*. Most of all, I am grateful to the 600 young women who took part in the contest. They are the heart and soul of this project.

Even though the options open to women and girls have expanded immensely, the number one issue young women still cite as most important to them personally is body image. Weight, body size and shape concern many young women beyond any other issue, including education, health, career, or partner choice. This reflects the persistent societal emphasis on what a woman looks like rather than on her intelligence, accomplishments or her character.

When we designed the contest, we left the topic of body image wide open, so that girls themselves could say what they wanted. I call these young women "girls" because that is how most refer to themselves, and I respect their choices. We expected essays on how girls' bodies helped them accomplish great feats in sport or dance, how having a disability or medical problem affected their lives, or how having a body of colour might feel in our euro-centric culture. We placed no emphasis on eating disorders, weight preoccupation, self-hatred or self-mutilation. We did anticipate some stories about these issues, and some reaction to unattainable beauty standards. We were, however, unprepared for the deluge of essays on these very unsettling concepts.

So many essays divulged the terrible secrets of young women who hated themselves because they don't conform to what is considered beautiful in our society. This unattainable standard put these young women in conflict with their families, friends, school and mostly themselves. They took a big risk in writing these essays; many exposed thoughts, ideas and experiences they had never revealed to anyone before. Some requested that their names not be published.

Although the book is primarily by and for young women, women of all ages will relate to the themes of these essays. Many of my peers are still struggling to accept themselves. We realize that the patterns of behaviour and self-criticism that we continue to deal with started when we were the same age as these young writers. I know many women who lost themselves in their youth and believed themselves unworthy of happiness because they did not project the "right image". It is exciting to read the words of young women who are defying the notion of the body perfect, and who are on the road to self-acceptance. They have much to teach us all.

Preface

Through this book, we hope to establish dialogue on an issue that is terribly important to young women, and has an impact on their everyday lives and their hopes for the future. We hope the book and its resources will give you the tools to begin this dialogue in your school, community and home.

Catherine Boldt
CRIAW President, 1998-1999

INTRODUCTION

"It's never easy to be the first one to speak up. My essay revealed my insecurities about my appearance, the anorexic tendencies I once had, and an incident in which I was sexually assaulted on a city bus. I envisioned that my family and friends would be ashamed of me. My grandmother...instead of being ashamed responded by telling the story of how she had been sexually assaulted time and time again by her boss when she was a young woman, [but] she never found the courage to speak up and tell someone. A friend at work confided that she had struggled with both anorexia and bulimia.

We all share similar experiences as girls and women. I felt powerful in breaking my own silence.... [helping] my grandmother and friend to break their silence, and in having touched women on the board [of CRIAW]." So writes Anna Humphrey, a 19-year-old woman, on winning the competition "It's Your Body, Write on it."

Canadian Research Institute for the Advancement of Women board members from across Canada had consistently expressed concern over the preoccupation of young women with body image. We talked about how the media reflect norms and values that lead many young women to believe that their bodies are the most significant aspect of their beings, that appearance is more important than any other quality. As feminists we bemoaned the lack of emphasis on education, careers, spiritual/personal development, physical activity, health, community participation, and self-acceptance for young women. In the fall of 1998 CRIAW, in collaboration with *Chatelaine*, launched a competition for young women entitled "It's Your Body, Write on it."

Board members and staff were infuriated that women are surrounded by unrealistic and narrow standards of beauty and personal appearance. We at CRIAW did not want to impose, like the media, our own values and beliefs on others or speak on their behalf. We wanted to hear from young women themselves about how they relate to their own bodies and what issues most concern them.

In the summer of 1998, an advertisement announcing the competition invited "young women to write on the topic of body image and self-esteem." The advertisement noted: "We want to know what young women think about peer pressure, the media, eating disorders, sport, relationship, diet, health, and fashion and how all of these things impact on their feelings of self worth." We received 600 entries and divided them up into two by age; between 13-15 and 16-19 years of age. These entries were then assessed by panels of women across Canada, including CRIAW board members, young women, and others. Sixty of the entries were selected and sent to *Chatelaine*, where a panel of four women made the final selection.

Anna Humphrey's essay "Self-portrait of an eighteen year old girl-Inside/out" won in the 16-19 age group and Charmaine McCraw's "The Dance" won in the 13-15 age group. Fourteen-year-old Charmaine describes her feelings on winning: "The day

Introduction

I found out I had been chosen the winner I was astonished, speechless, and even confused.... I was amazed ...at my accomplishment. I felt proud."

In November 1998 Anna read her essay about her ordeal with anorexia at the awards ceremony. She concluded: " I would . . . hang my painting [of myself] in plain view; in a place I would pass at least once a day, and eventually, I would learn not to be ashamed, and eventually, I would learn to see myself exactly as I am, and eventually, I would learn to admit that parts of me are beautiful." There was not a single dry eye in the audience. We gazed, stunned, at the beautiful young woman in front of us and could barely imagine how she had once despised her body and herself so much.

"I write to keep in touch with myself. This is a dream that I intend to fulfill," writes Charmaine. Her essay "The Dance" describes the "overwhelming feeling of joy" she feels when her body responds naturally to the rhythm of music: "My body just took off. The drums ran through my body and the energy was flowing. Each time I caressed the ground with my feet I rose higher and higher. Soon I felt an exhilaration that I had never felt before. It felt as if I were going to touch the sky. The faster the drums went the faster and harder I danced..... my soul...would not let me stop."

Joy and happiness such as Charmaine expressed were unfortunately few and far between. The essays tended to focus on the despair of young women with bodies that demanded food and could not be disciplined into submission. Women expressed horrifying efforts to starve themselves so they could resemble anorexic models and actresses. Anna writes of the "remembrance of the eight months spent trying to shrink away on plain rice and multivitamins, and water; the day the body gave out in science class, and the pulse slowed to near nothing, the lies told to the ambulance attendants, saying it must have been the fumes from the previous class's dissection." Other women became depressed when their breasts began to grow while others mutilated their bodies in anger.

The odyssey of suffering described in the essays shocked and touched us; these women reminded us of friends, daughters, sisters, mothers, and ourselves. We found some solace in the very personal and painful stories about finally overcoming anorexia, bulimia, depression, and self-hatred. Some of the young women found that simply writing the essay helped to break the silence and find a voice.

CRIAW is pleased to act as a link between these young women writers and other young women, teachers, parents, and organizations. In putting together this volume of essays, CRIAW pays tribute to the strength and wisdom of young women coping with the myths and expectations that degrade their bodies and harm their spirits. The struggles and successes of young women to love themselves, nurture their bodies and souls, and to be whatever they want to be, inspire us all.

Vijay Agnew
CRIAW Board member

Voices of young women

16 to 19

Art

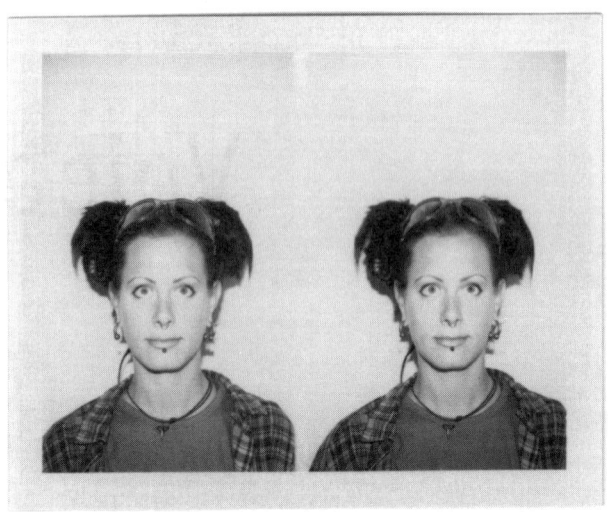

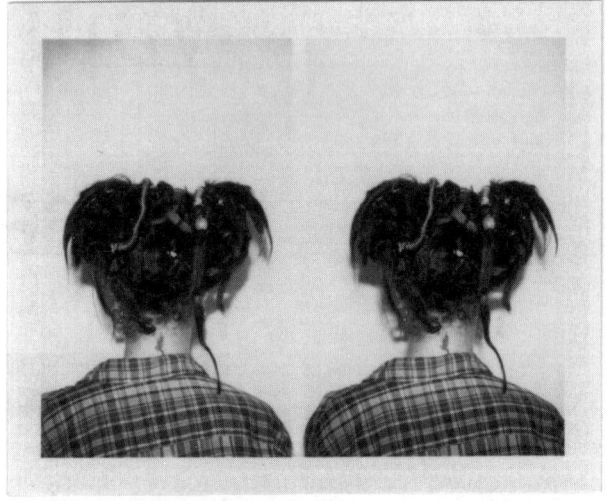

by Stéphanie Thanase Finnie

Hair

Winning Essay

SELF-PORTRAIT OF AN EIGHTEEN YEAR OLD GIRL-INSIDE\OUT
by Anna Humphrey

I would paint myself naked, in more than one way:

I would start with a pencil outline; a small frame, of medium height, with average proportions.

She could be any girl.

Next, I'd mix a skin tone (a pale one). Each imperfection would be accounted for: every broken blood vessel, acne scar, the persistent shine on the tip of the nose. The hair, I would do carefully, setting each strand in place with a fine brush in the extreme shade of red squeezed from a bottle.

She would start to look as though we might be related.

Next, the eyes because they're brightest. I would paint them without any mascara, pencil lines, or pink eyeshadow. They're small, but very blue. Then, the smile. I would paint here with quick strokes; light strokes, because the cheeks lift up and the straight teeth show, and there is so much softness, and there's a tilt of the head. Wide open smile, friendly eyes, squinting as if looking at her true love in the sun.

I would mix up a dark shade of peach for the shadow in the deep hollow where collar bone meets neck, then the small round handfuls of breasts. You might think this would be where it would get difficult to keep the brush strokes honest and even, and where the paint might start to sting a little, as if poured into an open cut.

She would only be beginning to be me.

Really, what would sting would be the ribs. I would paint the sharp outline of each one, in remembrance of the eight months spent trying to shrink away on plain rice, multivitamins, and water; the day the body gave out in science class, and the pulse slowed to near nothing, the lies told to the ambulance attendants, saying it must have been the fumes from the previous class's dissection. Formaldehyde will do that to some people, you know.

Like seeing myself in a clouded bathroom mirror.

Next would be the belly button. I would paint it big and round, and in it would be a mother's face, smiling, looking up. I would put her there, right in the middle, because that's where she belongs, holding things together. A centre of gravity.

Winning Essay

Most difficult, would be the inner thighs and genitals - for the morning on the city bus, when a drunk man with a sandy colored beard, smelling sweet, like something decayed, slid his hand across the leg, up, down and under. I would go back to add one small raindrop-tear to her cheek - to remember sitting there, very still, for much too long, surrounded by so many people reading the morning paper, or looking out the window - there, with eyes focused forward- at a loss for the courage to yell for help, the way they always taught in grade school sex-ed... and it always sounded so easy, and it should have been so easy. I would cover the inner thighs with dirty hand prints- to remember the pressure of the man's fingers, the way they rubbed, the way she could feel them for weeks; way I still feel them, sometimes, because I have never told this to anyone before.

A near perfect reflection

Next knees, calves, and finally feet, which I would paint in a bright shade of yellow- for all the summers they've spent burrowing into warm sand at the beach, or else a deep, sinful shade of red - for the night I learned to dance the meringue with a boy who hardly spoke English, and 1-and-2-and-3-and 4-and we swept across the floor, and the music was so loud I could feel my insides vibrate with it, and nothing else mattered but 5-and-6-and-7-8

Looking at her might hurt me.

Parts of this painting might sting; might take some tears, cried into the pallet to thin the paint.

Looking at her might make me proud.

Other parts might please me. I might stand back when it was finished, to look at myself, and enjoy my delicate neck, my long fingers which are tapered at the ends. After awhile, I would find a hammer and a nail, and hang my painting in plain view; in a place I would pass at least once a day, and eventually, I would learn not to be ashamed, and eventually, I would learn to see myself exactly as I am, and eventually, I would learn to admit that parts of me are beautiful.

Essays

AROUND THE NEXT CORNER
by Kat Aubrey

All smiles, tanned skin, graceful legs, and bobbing blond ponytail, she walks - or rather floats - down the long school corridor. She is not at all oblivious to the openly appraising, and even envious looks the passersby direct her way. She greets these looks with cool indifference, although to some she might throw back a sly, knowing smile. Laughing at her good fortune, she swings open the bathroom door and enters. The smile freezes on her perfect face.

Two girls, around the same age, stand admiring their figures in front of the full length mirror. "I'm so fat," groans the petite brunette, while sucking in her model-slim waist.

"I know exactly how you feel. Look at all this flab! I guess it's no lunch for me again," joins in girl number two - a red-head Twiggy look-alike - and she too turns sideways to examine an almost non-existent waist.

The topic of conversation is dropped as abruptly as it was brought up, and the two slowly make their way back to class. She is left standing alone, the images of the slim waists flashing through her mind.

Her eyes turn towards the mirror. The mirror that just twenty minutes ago had made her want to sing, now brings tears to her dark eyes.

She sees before her a fat girl. Not only fat, but ugly also. A hand reaches for her ponytail - a hairstyle that seems now to emphasize her fat cheeks - and yanks out the elastic. The sun-kissed blond hair cascades to her shoulders. The sunshine that had bounced off each strand was gone. Her hair is dull, lifeless, and coarse. The hand reaches up once more to smooth the hair back, but its ugliness must be punished. The hand catches, grabs and yanks at the hair, and a cry of pure hatred escapes her mouth. The tears turn to sobs. Heart wrenching, desperate sobs.

The hands travel next to the waist, and lifting up her shirt, she examines herself sideways. The hands grab the skin, and pinch so hard that blood comes seeping through. The inner voices have started already. *You deserve the pain! You are weak. Fat, ugly, pig. Fat, ugly, pig.*

The hands now journey to the legs. *What big thighs you have!* The voices continue their mocking chants. The nails dig in and tear, leaving their distinctive marks. The tears continue to fall, and hands reach up to swipe them away. The swiping motion turns to slapping. Blow after blow hits her face. The voices never falter. *You deserve the pain. You deserve the pain. Fat, ugly, pig. Fat, ugly, pig. Fat, ugly, pig.* Each slap is more violent then the next.

Essays

She sinks to the floor, and the words that echo in her mind slowly begin to flow from her lips: "Fat, ugly, pig. Fat, ugly, pig." She pulls the hood of her sweatshirt onto her head, and wraps her arms around her waist. She looks around her. She *must* leave.

Opening the bathroom door, she glances furtively from left to right. It's safe. Quietly, she leaves the building, passes right by her class room, and out the door. She knows she will be punished for leaving, but it does not matter. Nothing could be worse then having people see her ugly face, and fat body. The feeling of knowing that they are laughing at her. Like they did before.

The walk home is slow and torturous. The voices continue to chant with each step: *Fat, ugly, pig. Fat, ugly, pig. Fat, ugly, pig....* Each word emphasized with the same contempt. Finally, she reaches the house.

All alone, she glances in yet another mirror. The dam of tears comes flooding once again. She throws her body on to the hard bed, and buries herself in the thick covers. Then, utterly exhausted from self-loathing, she falls into a deep, dreamless sleep.

But before her eyelids are completely shut, a sole question rings in her mind: "Will it be the same tomorrow?» The question, as usual, goes unanswered.

It is not always this bad. Sometimes she looks into those very same mirrors and a giggle bubbles up in her throat, and the chanters say, "Lordy child, you're a beauty!" But sometimes, it is even worse. She lies in bed for days - too full of self-hatred to eat, sleep or move from the shelter of the blankets.

It scares her. What if one time, she does not recover?

Next morning, she makes her way, slowly, cautiously, towards the mirror. A smile starts to creep on to her face, then a grin, then a laugh of pure joy. She is gorgeous! Her eyes sparkle, her skin glows, and sunshine bounces off each strand of golden blond hair.

At school, she floats once again down the long corridor, not at all oblivious to the openly appraising and even envious looks the passersby direct her way.

But the fat, ugly girl is always there. Even though she may hide - for days, weeks, months - she is still there. Waiting. Just around the next corner.

Essays

EL CUERPO ES MIO (MY BODY IS MINE)
by Emily Bodenberg

Mi Cuerpo es Mio (My Body is Mine) *Title of a much loved Spitboy album

These days, one of the greatest feats a woman can lay claim to is emerging unscathed through the sweet and sour days of pubescence. So many of us fall prey to the booby traps (pun unintended) that line this path marked by burgeoning breasts and hips (and the perils of cottage cheese thighs, a disproportionately large chest, or none at all, foreign body odors, etc.). This process, this magical metamorphosis into womanhood is so marked with shame that it is often taboo to discuss the intricacies of such a change in public. I recall feeling very detached from my body at this time, vacillating from feeling like a tremendous goddess to a strange, awkward creature. I had gotten pretty comfortable in my little girl body, with its scraped knees and sticklike frame, and then it changed on me with little notice and I was left to start anew, to get to know myself again. The greatest discovery that aided me in this process was the knowledge that my body only really mattered to me and that I had the power to make decisions that directly affected it.

Even at a fairly young, formative age, I was concerned, if not entirely sure of how I felt, about others' decisions that infringed upon my body. In a grade eight English class, I read a speech I had written about why I was (and still am) adamantly pro-choice concerning abortion. Instead of feeling nervous about voicing my opinions to a class of gangling boys and girls, I felt empowered. I was transformed from a knock-kneed, sweaty-palmed teenager into a woman with something to say, a woman who demanded to be heard. Many of my fellow students appeared befuddled that I would choose to speak on such a topic; they were unacquainted with or uninterested in the issue, choosing to speak on a beloved pet or favorite rock band instead. I now realize it was then that I took the strategic first step in defining my relationship with my new body, by expressing my opinions, by being unafraid.

It hasn't always been easy for me to voice my opinions about my body and my rights as a woman, and the greatest opposition I've come across since my womanhood came in the form of a pack of high school boys who violated me in a number of ways, mentally and physically. I had recently changed schools and was vulnerable in a way that was easily taken advantage of. These boys, one in particular, who acted as a ringleader, were friendly to me in an environment in which I had no friends. It was a 'friendliness' I had never experienced before, overt and flirtatious, and initially I was flattered. But the behaviour of these boys rapidly became less acceptable to me, and PE class became a circus of fake homosexual acts, lewd, whispered propositions and—what finally ignited me to act— repeated attempts to make contact with my body. Mr. Ringleader himself was the most touchy, initially throwing an arm around my

Essays

shoulder, but then his behaviour degenerated into full and close contact body checking in a game of basketball, and then, what he deemed as fully acceptable, pinching my bottom. The first time this occurred, I was so dumbfounded by it, I don't believe I even responded verbally. I blushed an intense shade of crimson and later kicked myself for my lack of reaction. Had I shown him it was acceptable to treat me this way? Had I sent him a signal that prompted him to this deed? All fleeting questions; I knew the answer was an adamant 'no'. When he touched me again, I loudly rebuffed his actions while his friends literally squealed with delight. Ringleader himself thought his actions should be construed as complimentary, that I should be flattered, and that he had the right to lay a hand on me, especially in such a demeaning manner. I had begun to feel like prey in a class dominated by these boys. The climax of my relations with them occurred when, some time later, a member of the pack claimed that I wanted them to see my nipples because I was wearing a white shirt on a cold day during a game of touch (how appropriate) football. Said boy leaned over and grabbed at my breast. To make a long story short, I went to a trusted member of the school community and was ready to act (without the help of my female peers in the class who were either too scared or apathetic to join me). Unfortunately, further adding to my sense of powerlessness at the time, several teachers and the principal dealt with the boys without my knowledge or assistance. I had wanted to do so on my own, the class had been nearing an end, and I felt that perhaps I could teach these boys how a woman should be treated. As far as I know, they still haven't learned. I, however, learned a lot from them. They taught me about my boundaries, and that I do indeed have the strength and power to bring about change, even if it is with assistance. I know that I will not allow my body to be demeaned or violated by anyone ever again, that my body is mine.

How much I have learned, and have yet to learn. My lip is pierced and I don't shave my legs. I don't need a man or mirror to tell me that I'm worthy or beautiful because I feel it inside, whether or not I conform to societal standards of beauty. I will climb mountains with this body. I will dream with this body. I will go braless when I feel so inclined. I will be unclassifiable. I will dance this body to the rhythm of my own choosing.

Tango. Samba. Jitterbug. Waltz. I will be shameless.

Art

by Joanne Rycaj Guillemette

Untitled
(front of naked woman)

Essays

No Title

by Alison Browne

Have you ever thought that life was just a little too easy? Have you ever wished for agonizing self-hatred or a low self image? Have you ever hoped for constant dissatisfaction? Yes? Well, wish no more! Now for the low price of only your self-esteem you can own your own eating disorder! Imagine the fun you'll have watching it grow from the budding young diet stage into full blown anorexia nervosa! With proper care and attention you will see your new joy blossom and grow. Eventually the two of you will become so attached, you will wonder how you ever survived without it. Commit yourself now and you can choose from a wide variety of disorders, from the shy bulimia species to the exciting purge/binge cycle. What a deal!

Eating disorders are quite versatile and are very easy to care for, but here are a few helpful guidelines for you to follow to ensure you attain the best results from this choice. Eating disorders thrive in unstable environments. This is an essential factor to provide your pet with, especially during the developmental stage. A stimulant is required to "hatch the egg" and many sources will do. Some of the most successful ways, as reported by previous owners, are by teasing from peers, sickly looking media models, or high expectations from parents, to name a few. You should allow your eating disorder a nurturing container in which to flourish; one with plenty of ridicule and harassment. A perfect kind of environment is a high school. There the eating disorder has many daily exercisers and enough instability for healthy growth. Warning; Confidence can kill eating disorders! This Is their number one cause of defeat, as they have no defense against positive affirmations. Be sure to rid yourself of any of this before bringing home your disorder. As well, eating disorders mature best with plenty of self-doubt, so always ensure it has a constant supply.

Besides a supportive habitat, eating disorders also have specific dietary needs. In order to to grow big and strong, the disorders need to be fed insecurity on a regular basis. The most nutritious meal include insults (from others as self provoked), the fat feeling, or comparing yourself to others. If your disorder is stubbornly rejecting its sustenance, stir up its appetite by looking at a clothing magazine. The Twiggy-like, waif models can make even the thinnest girls' pets feel they have more work to do. Eating disorders love treats and if the meals are getting a little bland try spicing up its diet by fasting for a few days. This is the favorite snack of almost all the species and they will be very grateful to you if you provide it.

The last tip to remember in caring for your eating disorder is that it needs a lot of attention. Like any beast, the amount of love you show it will determine its success. An eating disorder wants to be loved, and yours will develop best if it given lots of thought and sleepless nights. If you feel you and your disorder are growing apart, renew your relationship by spending some quality time together on a scale or in front

Essays

of a mirror. One of the best traits of eating disorders is their loyalty to their owners. No matter how much you may neglect yours, this pet will always be waiting outside your door for the day you let it in again. This display of relentless and unconditional loyalty is why eating disorders are 'woman's best friend.'

So what are you waiting for? With such simple requirements and with so many benefits, it is a wonder that everyone does not already have an eating disorder! If you commit today, you will also receive a calorie counter for free so that your relationship may grow in knowledge and fear of fat. Where could you find a better deal than that? Your little eating disorder is just waiting for you, so come get one today while supplies last!

Art

by Stéphanie Thanase Finnie

Photo: Tombstone England

Face – woman – stone
aged by time
tarnished environment
crying tears
slanted by years...

Essays

THE SCULPTURE
by Gillian Burrell

Sometimes, when the house is deathly silent with the quiet of sleeping bodies, I slip out of bed and stand before my mirror. I turn on a small lamp and watch my pyjamas float to the floor near my feet. Softly I tiptoe to the door and ease it closed, leaving me silently alone with the smooth expanse of my body. Touching softly, almost lovingly the secret parts of my body which make me who I am, I am in awe that this body can evoke such wonder and mystery even though it is my own. My figure reflected in the mirror is much the same as a sculpture one would view in a gallery somewhere, simply because each body is incomparable.

I reach up and touch my face, tracing the curve of my lips, the round, gentle lines of my cheeks, the crease in the outer corner of my eyes. Closing my eyes I can feel the thin membrane of my eyelids. The body reflected in the full length mirror is so beautiful! Is it really my own? The tender flesh of my seventeen year old body intrigues me. How have those seventeen years sculpted the figure reflected in the mirror? What will my future lovers think of me? How will seventeen more years change me? All these thoughts fill my mind as I carefully caress each hollow, each fold, each tiny crease.

Gently I focus my attention on my growing breasts, so high and far apart because they are free of old age and the touch of a lifetime. I am reminded of the time a friend and I tried to find out whether breasts float in water or not. Cool winter air stirs the delicate skin and a ripple of goose bumps harden my nipples. My heart beat! If I stand totally still, a tiny movement can be seen just below my left breast. Then I blink and the faint fluttering is gone from sight. My attention is drawn upwards again. Slowly, surely I trace a circle around the swell, feeling the skin wrinkle and draw. Now my hands are splayed across my abdomen. The tension of muscles quiver beneath the touch, portraying a feeling of strength I did not know I possessed. Here my body gently curves. When I breath in, my navel stretches upwards. Breathing makes my hips jut out in stark, angular contrast to the soft, flowing lines of the rest of my body. I can feel the hourglass shape of my waist when I run my hands down my sides and a shiver of pleasure goes through me. The fingers dancing over each surface tickle and send a buzzing to my ears. I close my eyes.

As I close my eyes, my fingers find the mass of curls between my legs. An "arrow shape," I once read somewhere, "to point the way for unknowing men." Is this true, I wonder? Slippery folds lie beneath the curls, the sensitive skin hidden from view. I pass my hand over these folds and withdraw. My fingers are too cold for such secret places.

Slowly I turn around until my back is reflected in the mirror. A current of air slips through the crack in the door and I watch in fascination as the skin on my back rises.

Essays

The long groove of my spine is fitted perfectly to my fingers. I can feel my shoulder blades press together when I stretch, making my back wrinkle.

I open my eyes and look in the mirror once again. Buttery light from the lamp is casting disfigured shadows across my body, and I appear to be swaying. On the tips of my toes I stretch tall, reaching, reaching for the ceiling. My arms create a halo over my head. My hair falls forwards, framing my face in tangled reddish locks. With shining eyes that seem to absorb the light, I turn around and around, whirling to some inner music. I am myself! I want to shout. Look at me, this body is a sculpture like no other here on earth. It is unique!

I lie down and stretch across the cool floor. Waves of sensation ebb and flow like a tide through me, my fingertips washing over the planes of my body, soft as a butterfly's tongue sipping nectar from some exotic flower. I am writing on my skin. My fingers paint a love story across my flesh and the image in the mirror slowly smiles. My body, unparalleled, is truly a masterpiece of creation.

The line referring to the "arrow shape" is taken from the book, **Voyager**, written by Diana Gabaldon.

Essays

A Short History of a Body
by Amelia DeFalco

I used to wonder whether I would be able to pick my body out of a headless line-up: fingers, nipples, knuckles calves

I am at odds with this landscape of flesh.

As a child black and white films from the 1940s and 50s enthralled me. The heroines fascinated me most: their elegant charm, beautifully seductive. I lusted after their prominent cheekbones and sweeping eyebrows, their long smooth necks and visible collarbones. Observing their chiaroscuro beauty, my own pre-pubescent frame paled in comparison; my own chest was a desert, nipples stranded on ridges of ribs, while my belly was a mountainous dune. Eagerly, I awaited the lengthening of my legs and eyelashes, wondering when my eyebrows would arch and my chest would boast cleavage. I was impatient to become a "woman": soft, slender and beautiful.

Puberty came, and went, leaving me confused and disappointed. The delicate " feminine" flow is not innate. My cheeks remained full, while the rest of my body swelled as if to rival their curves. My breasts bloated, but so too did my thighs and belly. I discovered the scars of physical maturity in the spidery stretch marks which veined my thighs.

My sugary expectations were slowly dissolved by a vinegar reality. Somehow I had disregarded the multitude of "real" women who I witnessed everyday, women who were not porcelain and silk, but rather folds of flesh, tangles of hair. I had overlooked the daily faces, pockmarked and flaky, hairy and deeply creased.

The fact that I had not grown into a "beauty" appalled me. Desirable women are "pretty and smart". Bereft of physical value, I concentrated on the brain half of the equation. I waged war against my form, took my skin prisoner and kept it hidden under layers of cloth, adding to its detestable bulk. My own domination imprisoned me. Oh to be attractive; I longed to arouse. But who? Ultimately I longed to attract myself so that I might look tenderly on my own skin, that I would proudly claim its hollows and curves. But the movies, the television, the school, the people, the life I led, deceived me into believing lush bodies signaled defeat, surrender. An emaciated frame is victorious. (I have only recently begun to unravel this twisted logic.)

All flesh is excess; this body is politics.

Every female experiences the trauma of girl to woman. Our metamorphosis is more overwhelming than the caterpillars. They flower, blooming into a work of art to lightly fly away from that overworked metaphor of a broken cocoon; we wilt closer to the

Essays

earth. Trading corners for curves seemed nasty at the time, my edges no longer fit into the spaces allotted; I bulged in the wrong places. Expecting the freedom of wings, instead I was shackled, by my swollen hips, rounded belly. Gravity became dangerous (I saw aging breasts), and chocolate a threat. This body was an anchor. I bore the weight of my own flesh like a heap of garbage, foul and stinking, shameful; its hanging suffocated me.

I can remember the lowest point. It was in the spring. I was changing into my uniform. In the closet-sized bathroom at work, the floor waxed with pizza cheese and animal fat, the corners stacked with metal beer kegs, there was barely enough room for me to raise my arms and wriggle out of my T-shirt to face my own reflection: the horror of fluorescent-lit flesh, collected in bulges and folds. My epiphany: I am fat. Suddenly noticing with disgust the rippling stomach, I turned my back to the mirror, straining to peer over my shoulder - to view my shame from every angle. Shadows clung beneath folded skin on either side of my waist. Where were my ribs and back bone, my flat stomach, neatly divided by a vertical line? My breasts were not downy white, smooth. They simply hung, goose bumped pendulums of fat, marred by veining stretch marks, pale blue cobwebs of oxygen poor blood just below the surface.

Cloth was my defense, my weapon. Disguised under clothes without the tailoring of darts and fasteners, I tried to deny my contours, to appear a formless entity shaped by the layers of cotton. Imagining I were Muslim, I longed to drape myself in veils with only my eyes bare, wrapped securely in my anonymity. Over years those veils have loosened, but not disintegrated. Shreds of the bandages I fastened still cling years later. Nudity terrifies me, its emptiness. I still need camouflage. To shower in the locker room at my gym seems a Herculean task. Absolutely vulnerable, I would have only hot water and soap to comfort me. But I have begun to own this being, to be this body requires acceptance, acceptance relies on appreciation. I have begun. . . knowledge is the first step.

I know this body is politics. I wonder, do I exploit it, do others? Does my form exploit me, negate my intelligence, my value as an individual? I am not a human being, I am a woman, distinguished by my breasts and hips. In the absence of maleness is femaleness, yet, my body tells me otherwise. It whispers that it is not a form of negatives. Its curves are the original image, not a shadow. My fear quiets our conversations, but I am learning, slowly, to let my body speak, to trust its intuitions. The brain receives information from the core.

All flesh is unique; this body is a history.

The small scar at the base of my throat, a barely visible bit of crooked skin: a cyst removed when I was seven. Pinholes punctuate my earlobes, one, two, three, four... reminders of past decorative impulses. Sometimes, a glance at a mirror holds me captive, as I suddenly recognize my own eyes from photos of a half-naked grinning three year old, could that have been me?

Essays

Tangible memories, my body is a physical history. Virginia Woolf said that we look back through our mothers. I look back through this body. I share the mauve shadows under my eyes with my great grandmother. The moles on my father's neck and shoulder inspired the birthmarks on my face and back. Not only do I look back, but I also see forward. My future is not encoded in the lines on my palms, but hidden within my body's shapes and motions. I am only learning to use this vision; this body can inspire.

All flesh is sensual; this body is art.

I am the seam at the top of my belly, just beneath my ribs. It is a short dash which puckers when I bunch forward. I am the soft mole protruding from my left shoulder blade. I am the smooth creases which divide my belly into sections. 1 am the cross hatching of black hairs which escapes from the sleeve of my T-shirt. I am chewed fingernails and ragged cuticles, puckered elbows and arching calves.

Slowly, I am examining; slowly, I am learning: this is not a smothering shell I am condemned to inhabit. I have discarded the cocoon and have just begun to stretch my wings. I am my voluptuous thighs and round tummy. Why did this flesh terrify me? Even now I must occasionally defend myself against the stirrings of panic, fears of being swallowed by my own skin. But more often, I do not only inhabit this form, but it in turn shapes, creates me. What am I without my faint eyebrows and sumptuous lips, my wide shoulders and chewed fingers? Nothing. I would be you, or her, him, or them. The meaning is inseparable from the medium.

I used to wonder whether I would be able to pick my body out of a headless line-up. After study, I am confident. I know this heap of bones and tissues, I could claim it. But will I? To say: I own this breast, I am this hip, these lips, is a challenge. To be at ease within this skin. To own my body, to claim sovereignty over this landscape of pores. To mistress my flesh is possible. I am growing closer to possession; I can almost touch it. I will say:

All flesh is beautiful; this body is mine.

Art

by Isabelle Côté

Essays

GIRL POWER
by Laura Farina

Yeah, yeah, yeah, it's the Spice Girls. It's Sporty, Ginger, Baby, Scary and Posh. Aren't they super cool? Aren't they super gorgeous? See them wiggle, see them grind and yeah, yeah, yeah, yeah. 1 heard Ginger wouldn't bow to the queen because she was worried her boobs would pop out of her dress. I heard Scary butt-grabbed Prince Charles. Aren't they super cool? Yeah, yeah, yeah. See their concerts on Much, see their legs, see their movie in the theatre, see their breasts, see them sell Pepsi to a whole new generation of cola drinkers. Yeah, oh yeah. Read about them in the newspaper. Posh is marrying a British soccer player. See the picture of her ring. isn't it super gorgeous? Isn't she super gorgeous? 1 heard that she's really a man. And yeah, yeah, yeah. Hear their songs on the radio, hear the pre-teen girls sing along. 1 know all the words to Wannabe. Yeah, yeah, yea Ii and zigga-zig-ah. It's the Spice Girls on television speaking out about safe sex. The Spice Girls speaking out about safe sex to their eight year old fans. The Spice Girls practice safe sex The Spice Girls are safe sex, sex, sexy, sex, Posh, Ginger, Sporty, Scary and Baby yeah, yeah, yeah, oh yeah, it's the Spice Girls.

I am shopping for a bra with my mother and this shouldn't bother me the way it does. But I am thirteen and breasts are new and I am afraid someone will notice that mine are lopsided. I would like to get out of here as quickly as possible. I would at least like to get out of here before my father finishes looking at scroll saws in the hardware section of Eaton's and comes to look for us. My mother has called a saleswoman over. "It's her first bra," she explains and the saleswoman smiles, pulls out a tape measure. Oh my God, I don't want her touching me *there*. Am I blushing? I look towards the escalator. Isn't that Dad's coat coming down? "This is a nice frilly one," my mother says. I don't want to wear a bra. I definitely don't want to wear a bra with bows, but anything to get out of here. Anything at all. My mother comes into the change room with me. She watches as I take off my sweater, clasp on the bra. She is looking at my chest and the tiny bit of fat pushing over the top of my jeans. I am blushing again.

"It bunches funny," I say and it is true, these are terrible bunches of fabric around my nipples. My mother goes out and comes back with more and more and more. Bras with lace, sports bras, bras with bows, white bras, cream bras, even a few black bras. I am not going to wear a black bra. Everyone will see it under my clothes. This clasping, pulling, this staring is making me angry.

"I am not going to wear that ugly thing," I tell my mother and she looks at me and for the first time sees my embarrassment.

"This one is fine," she says picking up a sports bra, heading for the cash. No longer the fun shopping trip, the mother-daughter bonding moment, the coming of age ritual. Bra shopping is a duty to be performed. It is work. I turn and head for the book section. I am flipping through a mystery novel when my father finds me.

Essays

Yeah, yeah, yeah, the Spice Girls stand for Girl Power and that means they will do whatever they want, they will not let men get in their way. Isn't that super cool? Aren't they super cool? Sporty is my favourite because I like her clothes the best. Isn't her tattoo awesome? I want a tatoo. Maybe above my ankle. Yeah, yeah, yeah. Sporty knows karate and she can cartwheel. She won't let men boss her around.

My best friend's mother is a feminist. She goes to meetings and she posts literature on the fridge. She refuses to shave her legs or her armpits. "I don't want to conform to some chauvinistic male ideal," she says. She gardens without a shirt on. She believes in natural birth and herbal remedies, she believes that every body is beautiful. "Celebrate your body," she says. She sleeps naked, prays to a goddess whose picture she hangs on the wall of her room. The goddess is fat and glowing and good. I know my friend's mother is angry. At men mostly. Her ex-husband's secretary whose lips...but she says fuck him. He wasn't worth it. And she strips to the waist in her garden partly to show how little she needs him.

See the Spice Girls on the cover of YM. See the way they make peace signs with their fingers. The Spice Girls are all for peace. They say so in their interview. heard Ginger used to be in porno movies. isn't that super gross? Yeah, yeah, yeah. 1 would never be in porno movies. Ginger is my least favourite. Her skirts are too short.

In school I learn that a woman can be whatever she wants to be. The math teachers all think that I want to be a mathematician and the science teachers all think that I want to be a scientist, but what I really want to be is a Hollywood actress. I practice a Hollywood hair toss in the school bathroom mirror and I wonder if Kate Winslet ever suffers from chapped lips. Sometimes at night I dream of curly hair.

But sometimes, mostly when it is windy and I am walking downtown, I turn and everyone is staring because I am radiantly beautiful and they wonder who I am. Sometimes the movie director comes up to me at the bus stop and he says, "You are perfect for my new film," and I must remember to thank my mother, my father, my sister and my dog when I accept my Academy Award.

Pay eight fifty to see the Spice Girls movie. Yeah, oh yeah. it's called Spice World because the Spice Girls are taking the world by storm. They play concerts all over the world, but I hear they got booed off the stage in Spain. Isn't that super awful? I would wait in line all night to see the Spice Girls live, yeah, yeah, yeah, oh yeah. Do you think Baby is getting fat? 1 think she's getting fat. Pudgy Spice, that's what my friends call her. But the Spice Girls on the big screen is still super cool. I would see the movie twice, maybe three times. I would sing along.

Essays

FIGURATIVELY SPEAKING
by Denise Fuller

My hips are too wide, my chest too flat, my arms are too chubby, my thighs are too flabby. I'm too short....too small...too fat...too ugly...too flawed...

Messages about our bodies not being good enough for the 'social standards' set by bored middle-aged men and the women that stand by and don't correct them, is heard and seen on radios, TVs, billboards, news, articles, movies, fashion runways and magazines everywhere.

The result so far of the bombardment of "If you don't look like this you don't belong" is nothing but low self-confidence and self-worth...and in some death.

Cindy, Shalom, Pamela, Christy, Naomi, Elle, Linda, Bridgit, Amber...

They're sleek, they're stylish- they're our super model role models...a young girl's nightmare.

When you're thirteen and just getting used to the changing world around you, the last thing you need is the constant reminder of what you are not, what you and hundreds of others wish they could be but most likely will never become.

Why would you want to go through all the hassle of make-up shoots, hounded by press, no privacy, always in the spotlight never a moment where you're not the center of attention? Why would a young girl dream for that to be her life?

If you've ever been a teen before you already know the answer. You see the way your crush's eyes light up, the way he drools over Cindy Crawford. You've heard what the guys think of the ultimately beautiful Super Models in dental floss gracing the covers of Sports illustrated. They pay so much attention to a picture than they would ever to you- and you are standing right there within their reach, just waiting for the attention that they give the TV when Baywatch comes on!

After you've gone through all the normal thoughts of: Well, I'm not his type... I guess...I don't like this or play that or go where he normally goes. After normal thoughts leave, comes this hatred of yourself. *Well something must be wrong with me.. there's no other reason left - it has to be me.* You realize he doesn't know you so it can't be your great personality he doesn't like, or your brain...the only thing left for him not to like is...your body.

Sheena, Mary, Laura, Kim, Steff, Melissa, Jessica, Marsha, Susan....

Essays

You step back and look around you at all the girls who have boyfriends, at all the models with the perfect lives, and some sickening realization sweeps sense right from you. You want what they seem to have and you can think of no other way to get it. You stand in front of your mirror and grimace at your ugly body. Exercise comes to mind, so you do it... everyday, three and four hours. So what if it hurts, you have to look better in that bathing suit, summer's coming you know.

No extra meals for you, you are going to lose that weight if it kills you... which it just might. You haven't seen that far into your future yet, all you can see is the fattening sandwich you didn't eat for lunch and the breakfast the dog dined on as your mother's back was turned. You have to keep going, losing that weight...there's no stopping not until *they notice me*.

Your concerned mother asks why your looking so peaked lately, are you not feeling well? She thought she heard you being sick after dinner the other night, but of course your stereo was too loud for her to be sure....

In a weak moment you had eaten the most disgustingly fat meal with a dessert and knew you had to throw up- it would ruin everything! You indulge your mother a bit and ask her why the boys at school don't pay attention to you. Being the beautifully sweet and caring mother she is, she tells you not to worry boys are slow maturing, they'll wake up and notice you soon.

She doesn't see the tears that silently trickle down your cheek.. you know the boys have matured to the point where they're going out with other girls your age.. who are more pretty, more thin, more developed and more popular than you. She promises that soon they will grow out of whatever phase they are in and they'll notice little old you.

As you pass the living room on the way up to your cell, your dad and older brother are parked in front of the TV...watching Baywatch or Married with Children- doesn't matter. Laughing along with the sexist comments, making conversation over what body parts are defiantly real, not silicone. They'll never change. You give yourself a mental shake, going up stairs to throw up again and do 500 crunches. You're almost there...the scale says 105 lbs for your 5'8 frame but you can see in the mirror there's still lots of work to do before you'd dare get into that bathing suit.

Rosie O'Donnell, Princess Diana, Oprah Winfrey, Janeane Garofalo, Rebecca Lobo, Cassie Campbell, Mannon Rehum...

You are rushed to the hospital because you passed out in gym class. The doctor looks at you and asks when the last time you ate was. You start to cry, you can't even remember when you last ate or what food tasted like.. only the acids that reside in your mouth because of the constant throwing up. You cry and cry because there is nothing else left to do, you've done everything- and you still don't look like one of them....

Essays

When you've lost the blindness that had you thinking only the truly thin and beautiful can exist in this world, you suddenly see all these women that aren't perfect, that are getting attention because they are doing great things with their lives. They're all very beautiful- inside and out, attracting the attention you seek. Suddenly the possibility that this could be you comes to mind... and suddenly the image in the mirror isn't as frightening as you were showed and believed it to be.

Essays

No Title
by Cheryl Amanda Gullage

"Dedicated to the ones who lost out"

I am not perfect. I never have been and I never will be. I'm not blond, though my hair hasn't always been its original shade of brown, courtesy of Clairol and Sun-In. I'm a few inches over 5'5, which means I will probably never be a world class gymnast, but then again my inability to tumble would probably have been just as big an obstacle. I'm not a flawless size three...or five...or even 10 for that matter, so modeling, or even squeezing into the clothes of Kate Moss and Tyra Banks is totally out of the question. My feet are big, my complexion is flawed, my eyes are large, my nails are short because I bite them. In the summer I burn and freckle, I don't tan. I am neither petite nor elegant. I am far from fat free and my pockets are not brimming with funds to purchase the latest fashions. And in all honesty, I'd rather it that way.

From the time I was old enough to know the difference between black and white, people would try to complicate things with the grey areas. Details that wouldn't fit as one or the other and therefore required the creation of a whole new classification. Beautiful and ugly. For a long time everything had to be one or the other. I wasn't beautiful so I must have been ugly and all my faults only made me uglier. With each new scar on my knee or imperfection that appeared on my face I became more and more unattractive. My friends were perfect. Their vibrant, blond, curly locks were much more pleasing to the eye than my thick, long, straight-as-a-whip brown hair- or so I believed. And so since there is a limited amount of things you can do when you are in elementary school I took to conforming to "the norm" rather than establishing myself as an individual. If fluorescent pink was the colour du jour I was wearing it, even though I hated pink. If two inches of make-up on my face helped me resemble my stunning peers then I became the Mary Kay poster-girl, no matter how much my pores screamed for mercy at night. If almost all the girls in my class had three earrings in each ear, I'd willingly let a licensed professional punch holes in my unsuspecting little lobes, even though I cringed each time I thought of the dreadful act. I'd become a sort of clone - one of the countless young girls who were afraid to be themselves, knowing it may mean being different and different is not normal.

But I was always different. No matter what I did, what I wore, what I said. I was distinct, dissimilar, unlike all my friends, as much as I attempted to become one of them. They did not always feel the same way I did. My face was not the same shape as their's. I didn't fit the stereotypical physical mold of a "woman". My body curved and slanted in different forms. We were totally distinct people with separate thoughts and appearances. How on earth could we expect to be alike? And when I finally realize that I also realized something else; I was fine with being different.

Essays

I am 17, 5'7, with light brown hair, and bright blue eyes. I am not a perfect size 3 and I never will be. My stomach is not concave, my breasts are not perfectly round and big, and amazingly, I have hips. I can't hide or mask who I am. It's too hard and takes more effort than I have the time to deal with. In my opinion, I could be using that time for more important things. I am a straight A high school student, on the honour roll, a member of our student council, and in countless other co-curricular activities. I write for a provincial high school newspaper and am provincial President of Students Against Drinking and Driving. All this while holding down a job and applying to numerous universities Canada wide. Self hatred is just a waste of the little time I have to spend on myself.

I know people half my size, double my intellect, who still have not discovered the grey area that lies between beauty and ugliness. They've yet to realize that beauty isn't achieved through fashion or make-up. It isn't even achieved through the insult of others. Beauty can't be achieved in any form. It is possessed by all. It's just a matter of uncovering it.

The person I was, or rather the person I was trying to become years ago, is gone. And good riddance. That person was a veil hiding me until I was ready to emerge as the true individual I am. I don't have to be beautiful to be perfect and I don't have to be perfect to be beautiful. I just have to be true. And that truth is perfection is an illusion that no one will ever achieve so I'm not even going to try.

I am not perfect. I never have been and I never will be. And that is just fine with me.

Essays

No Title

by Chellby

Six years ago, when I was only thirteen, something happened to me that changed my life. I was just beginning grade seven. I was excited, nervous and very vulnerable. Wasn't everybody at that time, in that transition from elementary school to junior high? I met a boy and I became his girlfriend. He was very popular, I felt very lucky. He started to control me and he treated me very badly. I did not realize what was happening, or the severity of my situation. He was manipulative and I ended up doing things I did not want to do. I lost my virginity that summer to my boyfriend. He was high at the time and I was crying uncontrollably like the little girl that I was. Too bad I didn't have the mentality that I have now, to stop what happened, too bad he didn't care that I was crying. This lasted for a year and a half.

I am a first year University student, nineteen years old. I have dreams and goals like everybody else. I want to travel, I want to learn how to surf and live under the sunshine. I want to have a pet pig and I want to learn from other cultures. I hope to write all my life. I will do these things, I promise myself, but first I want to love me. All my life I have been my own worst enemy. I struggled with a body image that was so distorted and so very wrong. I went through periods of experimentation that may have been normal for a teenager, but were too much for me. I developed an eating disorder and tried to cope with severe depression, sometimes unsuccessfully. There have been great times, best friends, traveling, success, and a wonderful family but underlining all the happy times, my head was clouded with confusion and pain. I have learned a lot this year, living away from home. Through this period of growth, it has suddenly become clear that my confusion and pain will not be satisfied with answers, but only through respecting myself and moving ahead. I always knew this but I was never strong enough to pull away from the pain and actually do it. Now I am. I can feel myself healing as I write.

I have realized how closely the mind, body, and soul are connected. For all my parts to feel good, they all have to be treated with care. The other day I was having the worst day, although every bad day that exceeds the last, seems to be 'the worst'. I was tired and getting further behind in school. Automatically, my mind working the way it does I started to tell myself that I was overweight and ugly as well. Recognizing the signs, I forced myself to do something about my negativity. I went to my sister's house as a little escape from campus. I drew a hot bath. I lit a candle and placed it on the side of the tub, then turned out the lights. I created a totally calm atmosphere, simply relaxing in the bath. I brushed my fingers over my toes and told myself I loved them. I touched my feet and said the same thing, then my legs and moved up my body. I treated each body part with love. It was wonderful. After my bath I was ready to tackle the real problem and get some school work done. It takes an extra effort for me to be nice to my own body, even when I know I need it the most. Growing up, if I was

Essays

having a bad day I would leave school and smoke a joint, or I would decide not to eat that day. I liked punishing myself. In some twisted way I thought I deserved it. I was wrong.

Lately I have had a very positive vision of myself. It comes to me in flashes. It is a summer day. I am in a clearing in a forest. It reminds me of a clearing where my Mom and I used to picnic when I was a little girl. There are pink and yellow flowers scattered here and there through the tall grass. I am rolling around in the clearing, the grass is tickling my nose. My face is alive with happiness and I'm laughing and laughing, forever it seems. I think there is somebody there with me, although I cannot see this person. Sometimes I think it is my boyfriend. I feel his presence without seeing him there. I did not realize at first that this was my vision. It is me being myself in ultimate happiness, the self that I am working to attain. Now, I day dream like this all the time. I am always outside, running or jogging. I am always laughing. I am a little older and a little wiser. In my movement I can tell that my body is strong, my muscles slightly defined. My mind feels strong too. I am laughing out loud, and in this sort of happiness my body feels the best! My eyes sparkle. I imagine that my body and mind are working together and not against each other. I am a carefree woman who has escaped from the ugly parts of the past. Sometimes, when things seem scary, it is hard to keep a brave face, and believe in my vision. "All in time", I tell myself, "it will come into place". I can't wait, I am so excited!

Art

by Maria A. Bravo

My body

Art

The   sculpture

This sculpture is a body (my body) with a face of plaster. I worked with the image of an angel because it portrays the idea of good and evil, and also of internal conflict. One angel wing is good (without pain and confusion), while the other holds the anxiety and chaos that stops a wing from flying or growing up. The sculpture may not be real in our normal human appearance because it has wings. There are many things we cannot see physically but are there, like emotions, peer pressure, fears and things we face everyday that are not seen by the eyes that we must cope with and understand. Individuals can be either good or bad depending on their actions and their state of life. Life is about finding and accepting oneself and the hard choices we all have to face every day.

Maria A. Bravo

Essays

ME AND MY BODY
(AND OF COURSE, MY BODY HAIR)
by Alice Honan

Even as I write this, I am mulling over my vocabulary, searching desperately for the most appropriate words. I find myself apprehensive of my tone, my style; no doubt this is just another example of an average teenage girl experiencing the age-old self-consciousness. I am near positive that every other girl attempting to write this essay feels much the same way I do which should suffice as proof, I suppose, that I am 'normal'. However, I cannot seem to find as much comfort in that definition as I used to; instead, it appears to be something of a paradox. It is also 'normal' for teenage girls to dislike their bodies, to obsess over fat grams and portion sizes, to restrict their diets. Somehow I managed to overdose on normalcy, I guess: I ended up in a psychiatric ward.

I have anorexia. I cannot wait until I am able to use the past tense in applying that word to myself; however, this I am loathe to do until I can be sure I have exorcised every last remnant of the disease. I was another in the parade of pale, wan, disappearing into nothing girls. I shrank, both physically and psychologically, a point where my family did not know me, where my soul was congruent to my body. I have first hand experience with every horror story on body hair, health scares, and even a heart failure in my repertoire; surely enough to satisfy even the most hard-core of ambulance chasers. All these, however, I wish to forget. Life is dark enough already, I have to accentuate every hope I find.

I have to eat a large Blizzard every day. I have no choice in the matter. It is *incredible*. Screw the Canada Food Guide. I am swimming against the cultural current and I love it. I sacrificed nearly everything to achieve this body shape, and now I detest it. I have no boobs. I'm barely even a woman; instead I'm more like a scrawny chicken. Just in case that in itself is not enough to disgust someone, I also have the body hair of an orangutan. A true pinnacle of female beauty, indeed. And as for the term 'fashion victim'? Ha! I only wish. I, the famed Vogue devotee and avowed clothes horse, have been reduced to a wardrobe of leggings and polar fleece, fit for only a slumber party. If that. Of course, there are thousands of beautiful outfits in Benetton and the like, only I am too skinny. I am sixteen. Surely I should be able to strut in something a little more compelling than Gap Kids.

Even if I could find a pair of pants that fit me, it would be irrelevant. I'm not allowed to buy anything until I regain something of a normal body weight. I laugh when I see advertisements for Jenny Craig and the like - I, just like any other woman, wish my size four jeans fit me. I still cringe when I remember how sexy I thought myself when they fit like a proverbial second skin - now I wear a belt to keep them from falling to my ankles. The Blizzards are taking far too long to do their duty, in my opinion. Benetton's new stock arrives in three weeks and I still look more like a gardening utensil than a woman.

Essays

    I complain too much, I know. I don't even need clothes for my present situation in life - I am the oldest person on earth still tied to her mother with an umbilical cord. I have to be driven to school every morning, and picked up again at 2:20; I had to bribe my doctor to be allowed any semblance of a veritable semester. On weekends, I find myself getting excited over a few hours of freedom; only a few, though, so that my various psychologists, doctors, and general entourage can be certain I have obtained all the required calories. It's truly amazing how much food my body demands these days; I am my own personal biology experiment: digestion in fast forward. I would give my right arm to go shopping, to jog, to ride the train, to stay up all night, to kiss my boyfriend. All the 'normal' sixteen year-old stuff.

    I was normal all along, even as I starved myself. I was normal in the fact that I avoided cheese, and butter, and felt guilty over an extra rice cake. Just another average girl, and somehow I became my very own traveling freak show. Of course, even the word 'traveling' itself is something of a stretch. Sigh. Even worse. I have become the world's very own stationary boobless, bumless, bony, boring *'bovine'* (soon to be beauty, you bet your ass!).

    How depressing. Three more weeks before spring clothes arrive. I think I'll go for a Dairy Queen.

Essays

A RESTING PLACE FOR PINK DAISIES?
by S. D. James

When they found me, just steps from the safety of the spartan bathrooms, I can honestly claim I was in an altered state of mind. Dark, wooded area. Long, swift, hairy legs weaving their way through the bush. Glazed eyes numbly riveted on an object in the distance. Some kind of savage mountain beast, no doubt. Who wouldn't have been emotionally disturbed?

The scene: a crowded summer campground in the middle of the mountains. Early morning sun rays were just out above the tree tops. Then, the sound of feet running across the gravel path broke the tranquil silence. Crunch. Crunch. An early morning raid on leftover marshmallows? Hardly...

From behind one cluster of trees and nylon tents emerged the mountain beast. Its dark hair appeared matted and greasy, and as its tall form stumbled forward, a sharp pink object could be seen clutched between its anxious paws. Crunch, crunch across the ground. What could possibly make such a disturbance?

Armed with a woman's best beauty buy —her $0.25 pink daisy disposable razor —I made a mad dash for the comparative comfort of a quarter-operated, very cold, somewhat dirty shower following a long week of tenting in the woods. Disillusioned visions of a soaker jacuzzi tub and foaming bubbles danced in my head, and a smile crossed my face. Towards my mirage I trotted. I was literally a dirty, stinking, mad man. Well, woman.

So no, the only savage wilderness beast roaming the campground was the fictional one of our ghost stories told while sitting "round ye old campfire." The only tall, dark figure lumbering out from the bushes was me, stealthily dashing to the assembly bathrooms, desperately hoping not to wake my camping comrades. And the only pair of "long, swift, hairy legs" were, indeed, my own. Oh, and how swiftly they fled.

Onwards to the shower, and to the world of hairless legs! At this time, having spent over a week "roughing it" with my closest female friends on a bonding trip in the middle of nowhere, I was a desperate woman. You see, along with ground rule # 1 - no boys allowed, we girls had also made a pact with each other to ignore our usual beauty routines. Ground rule #2 - no make-up, no perfume, no hair spray, and no razors! We had all agreed that, just for this one week, we should be our true selves, au naturel. Sure, showers were allowed (there was a limit to our eagerness to "get back to nature") but hey, we figured the hassles of shaving and plucking and waxing would take away from the whole point of this trip.

Essays

And so, this is how I found myself nine days into an otherwise wonderful camping trip with my friends. We gals had a great time getting to know each other better, and I must admit that it was nice not primping and "beautifying " myself every morning. As the week wore on, I tried to ignore the shaggy carpet-like hair building up on my legs —a feat that proved more difficult that I had imagined.

Somehow, my jean short cut-offs just didn't look the same with the two mysteriously foreign hairy legs poking out beneath, and I still have nightmares about my furry cacti-legs in my red bikini. The lack of lipstick and ban on hair spray I could manage, but something about watching my legs morph into massive fur balls repulsed me.

Why this bothered me, I don't know. In Europe, few females ever shave their legs or under their arms —I have no qualms with that. With me, though, it was different. These were *my* legs, my hair, *my* body. And the hairy legs were driving *me* crazy!

So, on the tenth morning of our trip, I did the unthinkable. Rising early, I threw on my shorts and a pair of sneakers and quietly unzipped the tent flap. In the glow of dawn's first light, I tip-toed to the back of our car and retrieved what I've always considered woman kind's best friend —the disposable razor.

Pink daisy blade in hand, I scooped up the rest of my gear and briskly made my way to the public washrooms. All the way there, great thoughts of smooth, clean, hairless legs shining on the beach taunted me. No longer would I feel like some sort of primitive furry ape, or, at the best, one of my hairier male counterparts. *Sayonara* stubble!

Alas, just as my mountain beast legs took the last step towards the bathroom door, my mirage instantly vaporized as the door swung open and I stood face to face with one of my camping cohorts. So fixated on the shower stall was I that she practically had to scream my name before I acknowledged her presence. And then, her eyes drifting to the pink razor conspicuously clamped to my fingers, she discovered my attempt at salvation — my liberation from the world of hairy legs.

Caught pink-handed, I had no choice but to confess to my plot and plead temporary insanity. My razor confiscated and promptly deposited into that evening's campfire, I was sentenced to three more days in a hairy prison. Despite my cruel punishment, I did survive.

Upon returning to a world of modern conveniences and luxuries (including unlimited access to razors and hair wax) I admittedly returned to my hairless leg tendencies. Initially unchanged by my wilderness week of bonding and deeper self-understanding, I submitted to the inbred traditions of unnecessary pain and undue time consumption for simple hair removal. Once my legs returned to their silky smooth

Essays

texture, however, I did use the entire experience for a little reflection on our culture and my unconscious, instinctive acceptance of tradition.

Why, I wondered, did I feel uncomfortable with hairy legs? European men and women find leg hair attractive, and accept it as part of their culture. Certainly, if women still grow hair on their legs after millions of years of evolution, it is still a part of the original blueprints humans were designed for. Why does our culture deem leg hair natural and acceptable on men but undesirable on women?

I have yet to answer these questions, and likely never will. Nevertheless, I still shave and wax my legs like most other North American women, still succumbing to age-old traditions that require the removal of harmless hair. On a larger level, though, I have come to accept stubble as part of my life, and am gradually building a tolerance for the very thing that nearly drove me to breaking a solemn camp pact.

Every year my girl friends and I set off on our bonding, escape-from-the-stresses-of-the -city camping trip. Every year we make the same vow to abstain from makeup and razors. Every year my pink daisy ends up as virgin blob of plastic melting in the camp fire.

Art

by Shannon Clark

Essays

THE INVISIBLE CORSET
by Sarah Jasper

I think of the restrictive fashions of generations past and shudder. I, in my "liberated woman's" thinking, consider the corsets of long ago which forced a woman's body into an unnatural shape, and I cringe. I think of the suffering they endured to obtain that exaggerated hourglass shape, and I feel glad that women today are not so restrained by their appearance. Now, I tell myself, we have allowed our bodies to be seen as they were meant to be, in a variety of shapes and sizes. But this is not true, is it? I then think of the constant influence of media and culture which insists on one standard for all; I think of little girls who are bulimic; I think about the money spent to look eternally young, thin, and beautiful. I think about the images of near emancipation we consider glamorous. I realize that the corset is still with us, invisible but insidious. And it seems to be getting tighter.

And what role has the invisible corset played in my life? I never thought that my looks decided my self-worth... did I? I was, by all accounts, a normal young girl. With my metabolism, I was always slim, and I never worried that I was not pretty enough. That is, until my girl friends and I started to approach the brink of womanhood, and our bodies began changing right under our noses. Now was the time of judging, worrying, and hoping. I thought I would look like a little girl forever; my legs and arms were too long and thin, my body was stick thin, and l was a far cry from curvy. I also had to wear braces, yet another torture to the self-conscious mind. I judged myself "unacceptable" and looked upon the other girls with envy.

Looking back in retrospect now, I realize that I may have been self-conscious about the new feelings that accompanied my new body. When I think about some of the other girls I knew, however, I know that I was lucky. I had the love of family and friends, which gave me self confidence and security. Other girls I knew did not. Some of them began to diet as early as ten or eleven, and the word "fat" had already become popular as a put-down for self and others. A few of these were destined later for a nightmare of eating disorders and low self esteem.

But the awkwardness of adolescence slowly disappeared, and I changed from a shy girl to an extroverted, "modern" young woman. Around sixteen, I realized that there were tools out there to transform me, and I embraced them wholeheartedly. I mistakenly thought that there was no need to accept what you were naturally given – not when you could become whatever you wanted with the right equipment! This lead to a period of experimentation with clothing trends, hair dye, curlers, makeup, jewelry, accessories, piercings, heels, underwire and push-up bras... I had, I thought, come into my own. I could feel as sexy and attractive as I wanted, and I got the attention to match. At this stage in my life I had moved out from my parents' home, and in a new city I had all the freedom I had craved. The nightclubs and university party life beckoned.

Essays

The only downfall was that as I placed more and more importance on myself as a sexy, attractive woman, others tended to value only those qualities as well. I was losing my value as a woman and becoming viewed as a sex object. As the attention from men increased, my self-worth decreased. I couldn't understand why... now that I felt I was prettier, why didn't I feel more respected? Weren't pretty people happier and more confident? Experimentation with sex also sank my self-esteem, because I never felt the respect and love that I assumed was part and parcel. My first experience with a caring and thoughtful partner was far in the future. Although I was practicing safe sex, feelings of guilt remained.

   Now that I have a few years on that confused young woman, I have gained a wealth of self confidence and acceptance. I have also realized that I depended on my appearance to be my crutch, and that I never put my true self forward first. I misused and undervalued my body. I now know that to *truly* love yourself, you must be able to love yourself when you are stripped of all artifice. I have learned to love my body as it is: because it is beautiful, because it is healthy, because it is mine. I have learned that confidence shows through in your eyes and your stride, and people respond to it more strongly than anything else in your appearance. I have learned that what we do in life is the important thing, and our pride in what we have accomplished. I have realized that sexuality is not a game, but a precious gift to all of us. My corset was the need to be viewed as sexy and beautiful, when meanwhile I didn't even like my body myself. And now, when I look in the mirror and truly love who I see, I feel the corset slipping off a little more each time.

Essays

No Title

by Candice Jwaszko

My body. My vessel. My mountain. My body is my tool. A gift given to me which I experience and appreciate myself and the world in which I live. A world that, thanks to my body I can smell, taste, touch, hear and see; to be one with it. I love my body.

I love every inch, muscle, nerve, hair. Not because I am a size 7, because I am not. I am a comfortable, beautiful and dynamic size 14. I love my body because when I break it, it heals me, it helps me soar with legs as my wings, and it gives my spirit and mind a host to live through. It envelops my spirit and mind, and together creates me; unique, individual, and beautiful me.

My measurements are two feet that carry me over mountains, two legs that give me strength to run, a body that keeps me alive, arms to embrace, and a mind to help guide me along my path. And inside this a spirit that won't accept limitations. All these measurements are mine. I own them, only I empower my body, no one can take that freedom from me. And so... I celebrate!

I began the journey towards my conscious celebration when I was 14. That was when I became first aware of feeling robbed of an identity, being spoon fed by the media what I should look like and not measuring up. An overweight girl struggling to look like how I was being told to look. Worse than not measuring up, I was unhappy with my relationship with my body. So I took drastic measures and went to the extreme to prove I had control, that I owned me, and I was an individual. One of the terrible downfall society puts on people is not accepting those who are different. And we are all so different, to give the unrealistic illusion that we all should possibly resemble and act alike is highly unrealistic and cheating us all of the freedom of our individuality. I knew I was in my body somewhere, I just had to find it. I started decorating myself with flamboyant clothing, I cut 15 inches of my golden locks off and dyed it every colour, often rainbow. I put jewelry where I wanted it, in my ears, eyebrow, and labrette (area between lip and chin). I started looking at magazines and T.V. and instead of thinking this was how a young woman should look and act, I started asking myself how did I want to portray myself to the world. I did every thing I could to rebel against looking like a stereotypical carbon copy media icon female. At the time, I loved it. It was a fresh start to discovering what I liked, who I was and to developing my own relationship with my body. Eventually, the dye "dyed out" and I no longer needed to adorn myself with jewelry to feel like my own person. I "cleaned up" and found out who I was. I now dress comfortably and in clothing I like and best suits my body. I still have fun, with wild make-up, and fun accessories, do crazy things with my hair, but it's portraying me. My body and I working together to allow me to be myself, what a wonderful system!

Essays

Then, I started moving my body. I had exercised before, but for the wrong reason: to look skinny. Now I do it to feel good and to have fun. I realized if I wanted to go anywhere or achieve anything my body was coming along for the ride. I biked the Rockies, kayaked rivers, swam in the ocean. Soon, regardless of my "not so perfect body," I started to like it. It pushed me to challenge my strength and endurance, and I found an unbelievable confidence in myself I was shocked at what my body could do if I gave it a chance. For the first time I felt confident enough to go skinny dipping at the lake. Not because I had lost weight, (because I hadn't) but because I was happy with my body, a journey that had to come from the inside out. I realized the biggest limitations are the ones we hold on ourselves. Our bodies are beautiful, efficient works of art, and I won't hide mine; if I do, I'll miss out on life!

My relationship with my body is a healthy one. One I had developed by ignoring the status "ideal" of society, and changing my attitude. I told myself that I will not cheat my body out of its destined experiences because of imagined limitations. I will wear sexy clothing and look good, not being a size 7. And if I want to dress comfortably for myself I will. I am, in my own skin, comfortable and have discovered new and different ways to move through life, physically and mentally. I will love my body before I expect anyone else to love it.

I would not change my body to anyone else's, even a model. Every scar and wrinkle on my body represents moments of my life. I celebrate myself by feeling alive. Running through fields of daisies after the rain, jumping in a lake and feeling the water rush over my naked skin. Climbing so hard that it hurts every muscle in my body, and I keep pushing until it cries for more. The sweet taste of someone's lips upon my own. I know for the rest of my days, I will celebrate life. I know I will not let female stereotypes harness my freedom. And when I die, I will thank my body for giving me the strength and the chance to experience life. I will accept me, and in doing so love me. And I do.

Essays

Body Image
by Madiha Khan

This was it. I had arrived. And as I looked through the airplane window, I noticed that it was raining. It never rained in May. It's not supposed to rain in May. At least not where I came from. But in truth, it was those raindrops that were symbolic of all the changes I had yet to face.

Walking from terminal to terminal in this unknown airport, I observed my new surroundings and wondered if I'd ever fit in this strange country. The people hurried past me, shoving me out of their way. Twelve hours of sitting in one place and feeding on bread and butter every half an hour doesn't put one in the most charming of moods. I held onto my stomach and searched for a washroom. After a while of hustling and bustling through the crowd I found my way into the ladies' washroom. While washing my hands, I looked up to check my face in the mirror and the image that reflected back at me was the biggest shock of my life. This was not me.

The reflection was of this really tired, ill-looking girl who was standing behind me. She looked like she was about to pass out. She had the darkest circles under her eyes, as though she hadn't slept in years. Her nose, eyebrow and lips were pierced. She wore this top that revealed her belly which was pierced as well. Her ribs were sticking out and if I had stared a while longer I would've been able to count all the bones in her rib cage. Her jeans were about to fall off her body; the only things keeping them in place were her hipbones. She resembled the scary skeletons that I studied to learn all the bones in the human body from my biology textbook. I'd always flip past those pages because the structures of the bones and skull would scare me and here in front of me stood a Xerox copy of page 62. I was frightened. I thought that any moment she'd lose her balance and fall on top of me. She looked terribly weak. With my hand still lathered in soap I moved and gave her way to the sink.

I was so horrified by her appearance that I stood behind her staring at her reflection in the mirror while I continued to rub my hands together. Staring at her was really rude of me, I admit, but this girl was a rare species of a human body that I had never come across. I was told people in Canada were different. And being in Canada for just an hour, I know what they meant when they said that. She just stood in front of the sink with her head bowed down into the sink. I wondered what she was up to. I saw her putting her finger in her mouth and I presumed that she's just digging for the annoying piece of food stuck between her teeth. And to my surprise I notice the stud in her tongue. I was sickened. I wondered if they'd soon introduce a law restricting the number of body parts one was allowed to pierce. The most drastic body piercing I was familiar to was the right ear with three hoops. I decided that people in Canada were obsessed with creating holes in their body. My thoughts were interrupted as she let out this loud groan and started vomiting. She then once again stuck her

Essays

finger in her mouth and vomited again. She performed the whole routine several times. I was disgusted and terribly frightened. I felt helpless. I didn't know how to react. I didn't know whether I should help her, call someone or just let her be the way she was.

In a blink of an eye the girl fell to the ground with a loud thud. At this moment, I was the only one around. I bent down on my knees to see if there was someone using the stall, someone that could help her. Suddenly this big lady and I mean big came in yelling, "For Heavens sake Sandra! One day you'll kill your bloody self." She slapped Sandra a couple of times across her face and then looked up at me. I felt like I was going to pee in my pants but luckily I had just relieved myself moments ago. She yelled at me at the top of her lungs in the most sarcastic tone, "What are you looking at, sweetie? Go to your mama. You don't want to stick around here." She was right, I didn't want to be in there another second. I ran back to find my family who was chatting with excitement. But me, I dreaded being here. I was so terrified by the ordeal I had just witnessed. My knees were trembling. My voice was shaking. I hoped that I would soon wake up from this nightmare and consider it a sign not to move to Canada, save my family and myself the misery of moving here. I even bit my finger a number of times to make sure if this was really happening. It unfortunately was. I was in Canada and somehow I got the feeling that I was to encounter several of such experiences whether I wanted to or not. It wasn't an option. I had to.

Several months later (after the summer) I joined school. I was excited. This would be my first year in high school. I was all grown up. I wouldn't have to iron my skirt and shirt every night from now on, because there was no such thing as a school uniform. For the first time I was to have my very own locker just like the ones Zack and Kelly had on "Saved by the Bell". I was a little nervous too. I didn't know whether the kids would be friendly or whether the teachers would be friendly or whether academically the school would be tough. On the first day of school I wore my new pair of jeans (that I had bought with my last allowance), my new T-shirt and running shoes. I had kept this outfit aside for several months specifically for the first day of school and it had finally arrived.

As I was taking my first steps into the school, I felt sick to my stomach again. I rushed into the girls' washroom. When I opened the door I was amazed to see the girls in front of me. They were dressed in clothes that I'd only wear to a party. They stood in front of the mirror and piled layers and layers of make up on their faces. I was shocked. In my old school (it as an all girls' nunnery school) we weren't allowed to paint our nails and girls here were in full make up. I had the sudden urge to run back home but I didn't know my way around the city so I was left with no choice but to stay in school and wait for my dad to pick me up at the end of the day. All these girls looked similar, they wore the same clothes, the same colours of coated make up and most of the girls had the same slender body image, like Sandra. I rushed out of the washroom, scared to encounter another one of those experiences. Because I was sure that one of those girls just might perform the same gagging ritual. Surprisingly I had forgotten

Essays

about that incident until that day. I always shook my head whenever Sandra appeared in my mind. Somehow I got the feeling; there were many more Sandra's in Canada. I began to wonder...what was she really doing?

The first few months of school took a lot of adjusting to but they passed by fairly quickly. One day, after school I walked over to the plaza to the variety store. Ever since I moved to Canada I hadn't bought a single issue of "Teen" magazine. I always read that particular magazine on a regular basis in Dubai. I stood by the magazine stand and searched for "Teen." There were so many different magazines. They all seemed so weird. I wondered why. Every magazine had this ill-looking model on the cover. None of their models looked happy. They weren't pleasant to look at. They looked tired, ill. They looked like drug addicts and most of all they looked similar. They looked familiar to Sandra and all the other girls (my peers) at school. All my questions were answered. Sandra was not the way she was because she wanted to be that way. She was the way she was because she probably felt she had to be that way. I always read these magazines so I could get an idea of all the latest trends. And if every cover had these awful looking models who were setting these trends then results like Sandra were not a mere coincidence but a mere imitation of the latest trend. It made me wonder what beauty really was to this part of the world.

To me beauty was and still is a healthy mind and body. All our magazines had models who looked genuinely happy to be on the cover of the magazine. They were happy looking models with smiles on their faces. And most importantly they had flesh to keep their clothes in place. They were pleasant to look at. Not images that would depress you and make you feel fat even though you know you aren't. These models were real normal everyday people. They were *beautiful* people.

Everything made perfect sense in health class. I didn't want to be there. I had learned enough about vitamins and minerals. I knew the essential nutrients and the meaning of a healthy diet. I was sick of going through this every year. I reluctantly attended health class. I looked at the various posters up on the wall. Once again those images looked familiar...they reminded me of Sandra. They were all skinny models who looked like drug addicts. There was this one poster that I'll never forget. It was divided in half and both halves had pairs of identical skinny legs-chopsticks, literally. But the one on the left was a victim of famine in Somalia and the one on the right was a victim of the latest trend. That pair of legs on the right belonged to the London runway. That day I learned about eating disorders, such as anorexia and bulimia. I then realized that these girls were suffering. They were hurting everyday of their lives. They couldn't help it. They have no control over their thoughts. These were psychological diseases.

That day I understood what every Sandra in Canada was suffering from. It was then that I realized the different perceptions of beauty in the east in contrast to the west. Eastern beauty is the more the flesh the better while western beauty the less the flesh the better. I am proud to say that I am neither fat nor skinny, but happy. Unfortunately,

Essays

us healthy, beautiful people somehow have no business of being on magazine covers. At least not in this generation. We are just overlooked. I have learned to accept my body the way it is. I do find flaws in my body structure-but that's just human. I have promised myself not to take drastic measures in order to seek the 'perfect body.' My body is one thing that is guaranteed to stay with me for the rest of my life. I have no choice but to make it my best friend. After all, as the moral of Disney's "Beauty and the Beast" suggests, 'don't judge a book by its cover'…'it's what's on the inside that matters,' right?

Art

by Marian Green

Weight

Essays

No Title

by Emily Lam

The days drift by slowly, muted. Everything seems to be a blur. Outside, the trees are frosted with ice and snow falls softly to the ground. What would seem beautiful to any other person passing by seems tragically sad to me. The past couple of months have been like this silent and empty. I feel nothing except my resounding heartbeat, a painful reminder that yes, I am still alive and breathing. I would do anything to end it here, to end it all, but the responsibility of living weighs down upon me every morning as I lift my wasting body from my bed, in hopes that perhaps today, everything will return to normal and I will be the happy, carefree girl that I once was.

I'm not sure how I ended up like this, a shadow of a skeleton at five foot four and seventy-eight pounds. I hate waking up and seeing myself in the mirror, bones jutting out where flesh should be, grey, hanging bags underneath my eyes, soft, downy hair all over my body. The other day, Anne asked if I was wearing blue lipstick and I had to say yes because I was afraid that she would find out that my lips really were blue, blue from the cold which envelops me every day, from the moment I rise to the moment I fall into my deep, disturbing sleep.

I am scared. I feel helpless, like a rag doll thrown in the corner of a room, set apart from the rest of the toys and forgotten by the world. I wake up several times throughout the night, terrified of something which seems to draw nearer every night, yet so gripped by fear that I am unable to scream, to cry for help. I suffocate and drown under the heavy blankets which are never warm enough, ready for the night to take me away with it. But it never does. It taunts and tempts me, whispers my name mockingly, and leaves me empty and spent for the next day. Fortunately, I have found a way to fight back, to beat it at its own game. Instead of succumbing to sleep, I stay up until the wee hours of the morning, and wage the war that I have to fight, against the night, and against myself. I light matches and watch the flame until I lose myself in its entrancing colours, and join the secret, enticing dance it dances. As I let my fingertips soak up its warm gentleness, I feel no fear, pain, or cold. I am safe. But sometimes the flame turns against me and becomes my enemy, seeking to hurt me with its scalding heat, leaving me abandoned and alone. I then turn to the desk, the dresser, anything with a corner and bang. Bang my wrists, bang my arms, anything, just let me feel....

There is nothing I can do. My mind has turned against me, my body has turned against me. I have turned against myself. People who once were familiar have become strangers, dangerous. I know not who I am nor what I should do. I am lost. Ironically, periods of relief are found in pain. The burns and bruises are the only evidence I have to know that I still exist, that I am real. I am not crazy, I am not mad. I am just lost, and terribly alone.

Essays

The above passage was written as a journal entry in reference to the depression which haunted my life fifteen months ago, during a time where depression had altered almost every aspect of my life, and changed the way I thought and felt forever. Instead of focusing solely on the effects of depression and anorexia (which was a direct consequence of the depression) on my body, I chose to write from a more personal, intimate, point of view, in hopes of giving the reader a chance to be in the same shoes that many girls and women are in right now. The mind can be, and usually is, the dominant factor in both women's and men's health. It can be both our friend and our enemy, but it will always be the driving force of life. If you are in, or if you know or suspect a friend or relative that is in this state of health right now, I urge you to seek help immediately. Don't wait and hope that things will change with time because I know that if someone had waited until tomorrow to get help for me, I would have surrendered to my inner demons and lost the fight against myself.

Essays

THE MOST INCREDIBLE THING I EVER DID WITH MY BODY

by Jennifer Mills

YOU ARE NOT GETTING A TATTOO!!! That statement was punctuated by a week of silence on the part of my mother. Many people would have surrendered then, taken Mom's advice and dropped the subject. Not me. I've always been told that I'm a very driven and goal oriented person and my mom had always taken pride in that fact. That is until a getting tattoo became a goal that I was determined to achieve.

Now don't think that this was one of those crazy, impulsive teenage girl things because it was anything but. I had thought long and hard about tattoos and how they are with you forever, but I had also considered the other side of them. They are a form of body art, which like any other art, if used correctly, can accentuate a subject, in this case my body. With that in mind I spent three years designing a tattoo that was completely original. It was a long process full of nixed ideas and possibilities, but I managed to come up with a design that symbolized me. The perfect tattoo! A tattoo that I absolutely had to get and that's when I started asking my mother.

She hadn't had a problem with my designing tattoos; I guess she thought it was just a "phase" and that eventually I would grow out of it same as I had all my other "phases." She was wrong. After being turned down flat I waited a month and asked again. Same response. That's when the whining started. "Do what you want! You can go cut your head off for all I care!"

That sounded sort of like a yes; in fact, if perceived correctly, it was definitely a yes. It's all a matter of perspective. Some might have interpreted it as a guilt trip, meant to say, "Go ahead, break your poor mother's heart. Why don't you just slap her in the face while you're at it." Others might have interpreted it more along the lines of an open-minded yes, saying, "You're your own person, I leave you free to make your own choices and go with your own instincts." After a moment's thought I chose to go with interpretation number two.

A month and a day found me sitting backwards on a little wooden chair in a sterile tattoo shop. My back was shaved and covered with deodorant and a tattoo artist preparing to apply the stencil. I was really nervous and clung to my best friend's hand for some much needed support. The outlining was excruciating!! I gritted my teeth and squeezed my friend's hand harder. At first, I flinched at the buzz of the needle and the anticipation of the pain to come made my whole body recoil. The pain was like a hundred knives being repeatedly jabbed in and out of my back. I had never in my life experienced such pain. Before my tattoo the worst pain I had ever experienced was a stubbed toe or a nasty paper cut. I wondered what could have possessed me to voluntarily subject myself to that kind of pain. Luckily I became accustomed to it,

Essays

experiencing a dull throbbing in my back much like the pain of a bad sunburn. Every once in a while he'd hit a nerve and send waves of pain shooting up my spine. It was those moments after prying my teeth loose from the back of the little wooden chair that I would once again question my sanity. An hour and a half later I walked out of the shop - the same person who had walked in but for the black and white tattoo nestled snugly against my lower back.

My mom was none too impressed by my tattoo and ceased speaking to me for a while. It seems she had meant for me to choose an interpretation that meant something along the lines of "NO". I on the other hand was ecstatic! The tattoo was better than anything I could have imagined. It was exactly how I had designed and it fit perfectly with my body, as if nature had intended for it to be there. I showed it to a few people but generally I kept it to myself. I hadn't gotten it to create a new image or to make people think I was a little bit "bad." I had gotten it for myself and didn't feel that I needed to put it on exhibit. I wanted people to see me the person not me the tattoo. I, on the other hand, have seen it every day for the last two years and still love it. When I see it I'm reminded of the strength that I have in me. I've been asked if I would ever consider getting another tattoo. I've thought about it, but always hesitated. If I were to get another tattoo I would want for as much thought and meaning to be put into it as went into the one that I have right now.

Essays

ON THE LAKE
by Larissa Mornryk

The lake stretched before us, long, thin and blue as Chinese porcelain. We stood on the shore, straining our eyes to the horizon where any minute a group of canoes would appear. My stomach shivered with excitement, I flexed my knees impatiently and my arms swung at my sides, aching for the rhythm of a paddle. When the hard noses of the boats finally touched the soft sand under our feet, the passengers jumped out and drove away in the yellow school bus that waited behind us, like a giant purring cat.

Halfway across the lake, I had already forgotten the feel of ground beneath my feet. Kneeling in the sheltering husk of a canoe, the sun beat down on me from an unclouded sky. Waves kissed me wetly with their spray. Sweat collected in the cracks between my stomach rolls, which hung like gentle cliffs over the top of my shorts. I knew that when I finally stood my torso would be covered in horizontal red lines, like roads on a map. A girl I knew at school wore purple shadow in bright half-circles above her eyes. She was a swimmer and the smell of chlorine followed her down the halls like an overeager puppy. Every other week she would poke my yielding stomach and exclaim: "If you gave me a month I could whip you into shape. It'd be so much fun."

I thought of her then, on the lake in the middle of summer. I wondered if she could do what I was doing; leave civilization behind for two weeks and live for days with nothing between her and water but thin, coloured plastic.

***

The island was little more then a rock jutting out of the water, covered in pine trees. We tied our canoes to the branches that jutted out over the water, and climbed the steep banks, tipping under the weight of our heavy knapsacks.

Later, I would wander away from the rest, and find a tiny ledge of smooth rock, perfect for sitting. I looked out over the lake, the water and the air dyed mauve by the setting sun. Behind me I could hear a fire crackling, pot lids banging as dinner was being prepared, the laughter of my friends, and the silky whisper of tents being pitched.

I brought a nail to my lips, wanting to chew it, but then pulled it away and looked carefully at my hand. I noticed for the first time the crescents of dirt beneath every nail. I wondered if I had any pimples, if my eyebrows had grown bushy and unkempt. I realized that I hadn't looked into a mirror in days. Looking down at my legs, I saw that they were unshaven and covered with the pink hills of mosquito bites. I didn't understand how I let myself slide into this state of neglect. I didn't understand why nobody seemed to have noticed.

***

Essays

That next day seemed twice as long as the first. We paddled across lakes, the wind against us, our arms pumping frantically yet the canoe hardly moving. We carried our canoes over rapids, across roads and through forests, whatever stood in the way of our final destination. At one point we got out and pushed our canoes up a small stream, the ground slippery white rock beneath our feet, water warm as a bath up to our waists.

My t-shirt clung to my back, the bathing suit underneath it biting marks into my shoulders. The familiar trickles of sweat ran over my stomach. My feet were pink and damp inside old sneakers. But I laughed and paddled madly like everyone else, forgetting that I hadn't even brushed my hair that morning. I drank water from the bottle my partner and I passed from one end of the canoe to the other, letting it dribble down my chin and onto my shirt, glad of its cool cleanness.

When we stopped by some rocks for a swim, I joined my friends in the water, suddenly not embarrassed to remove my shorts and reveal the stretch marks that graced my thighs. If the sweat lines on my torso where the roads on the map of my body, then these stretch marks were the rivers and lakes. At times purple, at times pink, sometimes even a strange, almost-silver colour, they embarrassed and confused me. I wondered where they came from, and if they would ever go away. I knew from reading magazines that they were not beautiful, though they reminded me of delicate calligraphy etched onto my skin.

***

The sun had almost reached the horizon when we walked back into camp. Our arms and shoulders were numb, new muscles crying out like babies. Many of us clutched our backs, others clutched their legs, sore from two days of kneeling. Someone remarked on my sunburn, ran his fingers over my cheeks leaving white trails like comets. I pulled up the hems of my shorts to show him the tan lines on my thighs, not afraid of exposing their size. He praised the line's straightness, its sharpness and showed me the white spot on his arm where a bandage had been. Biceps were prodded, backs massaged, stories traded like baseball cards. We were like veterans comparing wounds, free at last to show off and admire our bodies, none of us distracted by outward appearances. I was exhilarated, successful. I knew that even if people did not consider me beautiful, after that day they would know I was strong.

Essays

THE LOW ROAD
by K. A. P.

My body is my shrine although sometimes I'm not sure if I'm worshiping God or the Devil. When only 15, I made the choice to give away that which defines innocence. I surrendered to a boy for that one awkward moment of bliss that most believe to be the symbol of the end of childhood. Afterwards, sore and wondering what would happen next, I concluded I was no different except I felt I had crossed a large river and the bridge had crashed down behind me. I suppose I had expected an overwhelming sense of freedom on entering womanhood but instead I felt dirty, like the innocence was gone, so entirely different from the woman I had dreamed of being.

I wanted to be proud and free, and physically beautiful, for I believed that to be loved by others would make me love myself. And so I set out to meet the standards of beauty set by the media, and ending up surrendering to bulimia. I began throwing up when my stomach felt full or when I needed extra confidence. After a time, I threw up to maintain my body weight and create confidence, all the while the envious comments of others fueling my tendencies. Eventually, the bulimia caught up with me and depression stepped in. I would frequently feel weak and blackout, food eaten easily rising once swallowed. I began to fall; my grades, my strength, and my spirit. I had been weakened, my childhood confidence fading to a memory, so that I was no longer able to deal with my anger, finding it easier to take it out on myself then face up to others.

Finally, I stood staring at myself in a mirror and I saw blue under the skin of my ribs and black under my eyes. I wasn't dying but I was a weak shell of the vibrant girl I had once been. I saw that I was dead inside, and no inner beauty shone through. It had been concealed and forgotten in my search to find pure physical beauty; a search during which I had lost a part of myself.

I saw then that it was time to grow up on my terms and redefine myself outside of societal pressures. I wanted to be free, to stand naked in the wind if that was what would make me complete. I had grown tired of being who my parents wanted me to be and what others saw me as.

One day, I decided that I wanted to make a testament to my search for independence. This testament took the form of a navel ring I put in myself after hours of unsteady hands and overactive nerves. To me it represented an accomplishment that was mine only, and no one else need know of it. It's true that we shouldn't put our trust in trinkets but I truly believed that that circular piece of metal had changed me. And in a way it had for it was the first step that I had taken towards my revival. From that point onward, I tried my best to digest my food, which in turn raised my confidence and my grades. I knew what it was to be strong again. I could now laugh until the tears

Essays

fell without feeling that lancing pain from my throat to my stomach. I could run in the wind and feel the sweat drenching me with a feeling of victory as I saw new muscle growing over my bones. This time around, instead of bulimia, I surrendered to joyous abandon.

I can call myself a virgin again or at least a "reformed virgin", and taste the sweet innocence and promise of a kiss. But there will always be a part of that scared girl in her battle towards womanhood inside me. If I just shut my eyes tight and remember how lost I was, I become her once more. Except this time, when I open my eyes, the world doesn't seem to be frowning down on me. I am without inner demons now, the only pressures being those of school, friends, and family. Ironically, I am elated when I say that I actually have those same problems as the rest of my friends without those dark secrets to make me different. But I also posit that I have more than they do. I've been to the opposite end of the spectrum, where most innocent children never dream of going. And I've returned, learning all the while. I may not know exactly which direction I'm headed in, but I'm going to make sure that my body is going to be able to get me there.

Essays

A LITTLE BIT TIRED
by Amy Lynn Rand

I am shivering cold, and getting a little bit tired of shivering. I can't wait to have that steaming hot shower after being in the water for three and a half hours teaching swimming lessons. The moment finally comes, and I savour it for another twenty. In the change room I look in the mirror and smile, for the moment satisfied. Height: 5'4, Weight: 97 lbs, Allowed Calories Per Day: 800-1000. I will look good when Andrew comes home for Thanksgiving. At home I drink my diet Pepsi and talk to Andrew on the phone. Dad is pacing back and forth. He starts to time me on his stopwatch. I can't say what I want to Andrew, because I am afraid my Dad is listening. I want to run away, to Andrew. I miss him like crazy. I go to bed, my stomach feeling very empty. That fact allows me to relax, and to fall into sleep. I hug myself tightly, feeling and loving my thin arms and shoulders. I plan tomorrow's breakfast and lunch, I won't be eating dinner. I look forward to breakfast but not to another day without Andrew. I shed a few tears and dream.

I am starving for my lunch, and getting a little bit tired of starving. Finally noon hour comes, and I eat as slowly as I can, to make it last. I make sure I am the last one finished I can't stand to sit and watch someone else eat. It seems so cold in the school I walk to the bathroom. Everyone teases me about looking very young for my age, and today I see they are right. I love my innocent, vulnerable look. I look small and childlike, and I am not going to let that change. I am in control. Height: 5'4, Weight: 94 lbs Allowed Calories Per Day: 800. I drink 2 diet Cokes at babysitting and give the kids their dinner. I get home before my brother's hockey game is over. I am home alone, and I wonder what to do with myself. My mom has made some chocolate chip cookies. I can't remember when the last time I ate a cookie was. I start to feel really anxious I want to have one but I've already eaten my daily limit. OK. I can have a small one, and then I'll exercise for 15 minutes in my room. I have one, and it is so chewy and sweet and comforting. Okay, just one more, I'll run really hard. Before I realize what has happened, I eat seven cookies. Oh no, what am I going to do? My stomach feels full and stretched. I visualize the fat filling into my cheeks. I must do something about this. I'll have to exercise as hard as I can for at least an hour.

I am enduring a horrible cramp, and getting a little bit tired of running on the spot. Last night I ran for an hour, and now before I can eat breakfast, I have to do another 20 minutes. I hope my sister takes a long shower, so I can be up from the basement before she notices and wonders what I am doing. My cheeks are red and sweat drips down my back. To think when I first got down here I was cold. Four more minutes. I visualize myself as a marathon runner to pass the time. The bottom of my feet are really starting to hurt, from last night, no doubt. Soon the time is up and I drink three glasses of water. At breakfast I eat my 12 Mini Wheats and quarter cup of milk, but

Essays

really wish I could eat more. This bothers me a lot. I walk to the bus stop with my sister and wonder how many calories we are burning. I get to school and throw out half my lunch. Allowed Calories for Today: 600.

What am I doing? It is the reception after the academic awards and I cannot stop grabbing food and eating it. I am trying really hard to stop. Half of me says, "go ahead you deserve it, smart girl." Half of me is screaming, "you stupid pig, you are going to get fat." I get home, and when Mom is outside I grab the Mini Wheats and start eating them by the handful. I think I have eaten half of the box. Mom is coming. I put them away and frantically start to run in my room. My body is stretched from all of the food that I have eaten. My mouth is really dry, and my legs feel like skinny pathetic twigs, compared to my enormous gut. This is not good. I have to babysit in half an hour. I want to cry the whole time at babysitting. The girls must be disgusted at how fat I look. I don't want to play Barbies, I want to exercise. Finally home. I have a test tomorrow, but nothing is going to stop me from running for the entire two hours before Andrew calls. Thank goodness for hockey. Mom and Dad can't stop me. At first I am stiff and uncomfortable, my stomach and my bowels bounce heavily within me. I am extremely thirsty, and allow myself a quick gulp of water every 5 minutes. I blare the music to make myself keep going, I try to get my arms into the action, to keep them thin. I feel my heart beating fast and hard in my chest and my head. At some point, I no longer feel full. I feel strong and fit, like a professional dancer. I have unlimited energy. I am actually enjoying myself, I feel like I can do anything. I have my body back again. Eventually the time is up, and I feel relieved. That night I have a lot of trouble sleeping. My feet throb and my legs are stiff and sore. l feel dizzy and lightheaded. I promise myself that I will never make myself have to spend that much time exercising again. Height: 5'4, Weight: 92 1bs Allowed Calories For Tomorrow: 600.

"Amy, I am not going to allow you to go away to school next year if you don't start eating. You look anorexic."

It's Saturday, and I am home alone. I eat four bowls of Honey Nut Cheerios, two Poptarts, six Oreos, and I don't know how many spoonfuls of peanut butter dipped in sugar.

"Anorexic Mom, yeah right. Look at what I eat. I should weight 300 pounds." I feel like I want to be sick, and I try to make myself throw up. But for some reason that is one thing I am not able to do. I feel absolutely disgusting.

"Amy, what size jeans do you wear? You have no butt girl."

I lie down on my bloated stomach for a while and cry, I am so afraid to get fat. For the next three hours, I will exercise like a madwoman. It feels like knives are piercing my abdomen, and my legs hurt very badly, but somehow I press on.

Essays

"Amy drink every last drop of that milk RIGHT NOW. You are becoming a real idiot, you know that?"

As I run, I think that all of this compulsive exercise must not be very healthy for the mind. I realize that I do not deserve to be going through this.

"Oh my god, look at how skinny Amy is."

I have to stop before three hours is up, my cramps are so bad that I can't breathe.

"Ugh, it's so hot in here. Mom, Amy was jumping around again!"

Height: 5'4, Weight: 87lbs Allowed Calories for the Day: none, because once I start eating I can't stop.

"Amy, every time I come home you are skinnier and skinnier. You need to start eating more. I'm getting worried about you."

I wish I could tell Andrew that I need help, but I get scared and don't know how.

"Amy, What you doing eating that, aren't you afraid of getting FAT!"

There is bitterness in my brother's voice and I can't figure out why.

I feel nervous and weak, and I'm getting a little bit tired of feeling like this... When I first started working at the pool I weighed 110 pounds. Today at training I hardly have enough strength. The thing that carries me on is the fact that I am burning off the yogurt that I ate before I came. I feel like I don't deserve my job.

"You cold Ame? That's cause you need to get some meat on those bones!"

One night I wake up at 3:00 am and exercise in the dark for an hour. I am careful to not wake Hilary up. I am scared. I feel like I have lost my mind. Tomorrow, I must get help. I will talk to Beth. I will ask her to help me. I am a sick girl.

"Come on. Amy, lets go and see Mrs. Huntley. She'll know what you can do."

Mrs. Huntley does not seem surprised to see me. Beth talks for me, and I start to cry. I will go to a walk-in clinic in a couple of days with Mrs. Huntley. I love Beth. She truly is my best friend. I love Mrs. Huntley too.

I am crying again, and getting a little bit tired of crying. The eating disorder specialist tells me how brave I am to come here. She tells me I am not insane.

Essays

It could be because my dad is an alcoholic.
It could be my coping mechanism.
It could be that I feel controlled.
It could be due to the pressures of society on girls to be thin.
It could be due to a chemical imbalance in my brain.
It could be that I suffer from high levels of anxiety and depression.
It could be all of these things, but now the important thing is that I work on getting better.

Height: 5'4, Weight: 85lbs Allowed Calories for the Day: I'm not sure.

On a scale of 1 to 10, how motivated are you to overcome the eating disorder?

I visualize the past year of my life in flashes... Hanging over the toilet trying to throw up, holding my stomach in agony... Watching the girls eat, sipping diet Coke... Staring into the mirror and getting a little bit tired of staring... Counting calories and minutes, and getting a little bit tired of counting... Running and jumping, moving around frantically, despite the blisters on my feet. Despite the pain in my shins and in my sides. Despite my nausea. Despite my thirst. Despite my exhaustion. Despite the fact that I should be studying, playing, socializing, sleeping. Despite the fact that I am crying... Shivering cold... perpetually cold, and seeking a little bit of comfort.

I take a deep breath and circle 10.

I am running again. I am outside on a track, in my Sir James Dunn track team uniform. It is the 3000 m race, at the city meet. This is the first year that I have been in track and field, and I am surprised to find myself running in 3rd place. I have no blisters on my feet. There is no pain in my shins or in my sides. I am not sick, I am strong, and I am running like the wind. With one lap to go, I can hear my school cheering for me. I know they did not expect me to be running this well. For the last 200 meters there is a girl right at my heels, but I give it everything I have, and I win 3rd place. Everyone congratulates me. I can't wait to tell the girls in my eating disorder help group tomorrow.

"Amy, the team is going out for dinner to Aurora's to celebrate, are you coming?"
Definitely.

Height: 5'4 Weight 98 1bs Allowed Calories for the Day: this number no longer exists.

It only wastes so much precious time.
And quite frankly,
I am getting a little bit tired of wasting.

Essays

SEEING PAST THE MIRROR AND BEYOND MY BODY

by Rebecca Silver-Slayter

I'm not overweight. I never have been. Perhaps no one will listen to me, because I've never been one of those girls who wasted her adolescence standing on scales or counting out the calories of every piece of food I put in my mouth. These days, you can look through any teenage magazine, and read some triumphant story of a girl who was fat and lost the weight and became a 'better person', or of a girl who nearly starved herself to death, but survived and came to terms with her body. And on the following pages you see airbrushed, digitally remastered photographs of girls whose ankles and wrists look like they could break in too strong a gust of wind; girls who look too fragile to ever do anything but smile into a camera. I guess the world wants to hear these 'triumphant' stories, about weight, because that is the focus of the ideal body nowadays. But I am thin, and I am not anorexic, and yet the pages of these kinds of magazines and similar media portrayal of the body it takes to be happy and accepted and loved, have broken a piece off of me, a piece I may never fully have back.

When I was young I never gave a thought to how I looked. I didn't want to be a girl. I spent my childhood trying to fit in with the boys I played with. It was always foremost in my mind, that at any cost, I must always be able to run faster, climb higher, and cry less than any of my friends, simply because I was the girl, and any fault in me might cause them to see me as the girl I was. And so I ran everyday, and I swam in the ocean in late March, because it was always a competition to see who would be the first to brave the icy waters at the beginning of each Spring. I had to win every race. And that was all I cared about. I scorned all things female, and laughed at make up, dresses and styled hair. And yet, already, it had become ingrained in me that there was something different about me because I was a girl, and that it was not enough to just be me, but that I had to aspire to something else, something that would pass approval.

I guess it was when I was around 15, that my body as a swimmer, a runner and a dancer ceased to be enough. Ironically it began with someone calling me pretty. I had never before associated the word with myself, but somehow it suddenly occurred to me that that was what I had to be. I became more aware of people around me, mentally categorizing each as pretty or ugly. Before I had never noticed which friends of mine were pretty, but suddenly I began to look at them with envious eyes, hungry for the beauty I felt they possessed that I could never have. Again, I felt shut out of some elite world, but this time not because I was a girl, but because I was not beautiful. And this time it was a difference I could not make up for, not by running a thousand miles.

Every face on television or between the pages of magazines, seemed an insult directed towards me. These were the people I could never be, could never live up to. Suddenly my nose was too crooked, my skin too pale, my neck and arms and legs too

Essays

long, my eyelashes too short. Every beautiful face pointed out another piece of me that was somehow wrong.

For too long I drowned in my own shortcomings. My best friend and I would pull ourselves apart, horribly accusing every feature as being the cause of this feeling, this terrible realization of our inadequacy. I wonder now, looking back, if we really believed we were ugly, or if we called ourselves this out of fear that if we didn't, someone else would.

I can't pinpoint the exact miraculous moment when I stopped seeing myself as a body, and began to see myself as a person, because there wasn't one. I didn't one day look in the mirror and realize I was beautiful. But I did grow up. And as part of that, I began to love the person I was, and the shell around that person, became just that –a shell. If I look in the mirror I can still list for you a hundred changes I would like to make, but I don't look in the mirror all that often anymore. I don't need to. I don't want to limit myself down to being a reflection on glass because that's not me. I am a beautiful person who embraces life with everything I have, and I can't see that in any mirror, so why look at something that lies to me, or only tells half the story. And there are even odd days when I notice something about my physical self that is beautiful, but I don't dwell on that, because I don't want to begin the cycle again.

This is not a story of triumph, because I have not won anything. I have only gathered back what was taken from me, and even that is not, and will never be, completely mine again. If anything, this is a tragic story, because something terrible happened to a little girl who should have spent her time eating ice cream cones and laughing. And it is all the more tragic because it is not an unusual story, but something that happens to every teenage girl. They will tell you it is a part of growing up. But it shouldn't be. One shouldn't have to fall down first to grow up.

On the news recently, I saw an interview with a girl who was dying of anorexia. She couldn't have been more than ten years old. She was so breathlessly young, and already the world of mass media selling perfection and insecurity, the fashionable numbness, had killed her. She was killing herself slowly, deliberately, pushing away food; to be perfect she would kill herself and she was killing herself because she couldn't be perfect. I wept as I watched her, her tiny bones lost in the hospital sheets, her hungry aching eyes looking in the camera with this terrible fear. I wept because I know that little girl, I know her frightened eyes, I have seen them in the mirror. She is a piece of every one of us, the personification of all the terrible crimes committed by our own insecurities, that is brushed off as adolescent self-consciousness. I want the world to see, to truly see what terrible things we do to ourselves every time we stand on a scale or gaze into our own vacant reflections. That little girl was dying of hunger for everything we took away from her, or never let her have, and she is a part of us all. I wish that we could give everything we took from her back, and back to ourselves.

Essays

I love my body, not because it's perfect, but because it's mine. Because it can dance and climb mountains, and laugh and build tree forts, write poetry and play guitar. Recently someone told me I had nice legs. "Thanks," I said, "They take me where I'm going."

And that's all I want for us, I guess. To realize that our bodies are our own, and are there simply as the vehicle to the realization of our dreams. I wish that I could take the little girl I was who worked so hard, with such beautiful energy at being the fastest and best, and the slightly older girl who spent hours finding sadness in the mirror, and wrap my arms around both of them and tell them, "It's OK. You don't need to prove yourself to anyone. You are enough." This is what I wish that I could give back to the world.

Art

by Malaika Golland

Untitled

Essays

THE DANCE TO FREEDOM
by Pandora Syperek

I am a belly dancer. Yeah, you heard me - a belly dancer! I might not look like one, but unlike the modern doctrines that define beauty by body type alone, in belly dancing its not what your body looks like that matters but what you do with it. Through belly dancing I've gained control over my sense of beauty and of my own self image. Belly dancing has allowed me to dismiss the archetypal ideals of feminine beauty and to love my body.

It seems to me that there are three major ideals for women's looks. They are all extremes, and unless one happens to be born that way (which is very rare,) one must go to extreme measures to even come close to achieving the desired look. The first type is The Waif. She is as thin and as light as a sheet of paper. Airy and weightless, she floats around, placidly and vacantly. She is ethereal. The only thing covering her exquisite little bones is a thin layer of pure, white skin, and she is visibly fragile and delicate, even frail. At the same time though, The Waif resembles a pre-pubescent, what with her child-like innocence and naiveté, and with her virginal complexion. Examples of the Waif include Twiggy, Kate Moss, and many modern fashion models as well as starving children in Ethiopia.

The second type of woman is very different than the first but is as extreme in her genre. She is The Hourglass. She is buxom and curvaceous. Voluptuous and seductive, she flaunts around, alluringly and bewitchingly. She is built like a house. She is ultra-womanly and ridiculously feminine, and though she is soft, cushy and warm, The Hourglass remains an enchanting and tantalizing siren. Examples of The Hourglass include Marilyn Monroe, any Baywatch actress (especially when Pammy was on it) and the Fredericks of Hollywood models, as well as porn stars and cartoon characters.

The third ideal is the most modem and supposedly the healthiest. She is The Stairmaster. She is stretched, toned, built and defined. Cheery and energetic, she bounces around, vibrantly and tirelessly. She is effervescent. Fit and fat-free, The Stairmaster is liberated from any embarrassingly feminine curves or bulges, save the breasts she carries high above her rippling, washboard abs, which appear to just be some extra, very round, perky muscles with nipples in their centres. She is loaded with self-control and discipline, yet she manages to be exuberant and vivacious. Examples of The Stairmaster include women in health club ads, Linda Hamilton in Terminator 2, and Jane Fonda, as well as fourteen year old Olympic gymnasts.

Okay, so I lied. There are more than three types of women, but I'm not really sure one can even call the fourth type a woman, since she is so tremendous, so extraordinary, and so phenomenal (not to mention implausible) that she almost seems super-natural. She is The Paramount of feminine beauty. She combines the delicate,

Essays

diaphanous grace of The Waif (she is a toothpick;) the foxy, shapely sensuality of The Hourglass (she is stacked;) and the ebullient, wholesome buoyancy of The Stairmaster (she's got a buff bod.) This is the look of such supermodels as Cindy Crawford and Claudia Schiffer, and you can catch a glimpse of this epitome of feminine beauty in the Victoria's Secret catalogue. Though many women would love to reach these great heights of perfection, the majority of them simply don't have a chance. In order to achieve them, most women would have to resort to pretty extreme measures, such as starvation, surgery, or moving into the gym.

The first time I saw my belly dance teacher, I thought, great, another impossible ideal to strive for. Tahia had a large, powerful bustline, a defined waist, shapely hips and rear, and of course the quintessential perfectly round and feminine belly. Bosomy and soft, yet robust and matriarchal, Tahia made me look like a scrawny little stick figure. I realized that everything that stops me from looking like a model isn't prominent enough for me to look like a belly dancer. Go figure. Then something amazing happened. One day I came to class to find that one of Tahia's advanced students, Katie, was filling in for her. I couldn't believe my eyes - Katie was skinny! Not model-skinny, but kind of like me - slim yet shapely. And she could dance, Man! Of course, with such a different body from Tahia, the effect was quite different, but not any less lovely, graceful, or sensuous. Upon this realization, I looked around at my class and discovered something else: The women's bodies had nothing to do with how well they danced. In fact, the girl who had the most traditional belly dancer body happened to be the worst dancer in the class! This was when I first fully realized that in belly dance, it's not what your body looks like that matters but what you do with it.

When I dance I can be everything. Such walks as the horse trot are tight, controlled, and exquisite, whereas other more slinky moves, such as the undulation or snake arms, are more continuous, liquid, and seductive. Hip figure eights accentuate the curve of the hips and are gooey and enticing, while the chest movements we do isolate and emphasize the bust yet, when performed properly, look good no matter how small one's cup size is. Finally, there's the shimmy, which can be combined with many moves to add playfulness, bounce and exuberance - kind of like The Stairmaster, except real. Within one dance, I can exhibit all these different moods and attitudes! Dancing makes me feel beautiful, sexy, and powerful.

Through belly dancing I learned that no matter what your body looks like, it's what you do with it that's important. You can be whatever you want if you just take control instead of letting others' ideas rule your self image. Only this can truly make you feel attractive. Because in the end, it's how you feel about your body that really matters.

Essays

No Title

by Jessica Wilford

Standing alone in the bathroom, I gripped the stainless steel ring implanted in my navel with two pairs of pliers, and wrenched until the bead popped out, leaving a gap in the center of the fourteen gauge ring. With a little difficulty, I freed the ring from my skin, leaving behind two inflamed red holes, one above and one just inside my bellybutton.

That was about a month ago, when I'd had my bellybutton pierced for two months. After much persuading, my parents had finally agreed that at 17, I was old enough to get a piercing. Contrary to what some might assume, piercing my navel was not at all about rebelling against my parents or impressing my friends. At the time, I felt I was doing it only for myself. As I lay on the piercer's table and felt the sharp pain of the needle followed by the tug of the ring, a strange exhilaration flowed through me. I felt as though I was asserting my claim over my own body, proving my control over it.

During the time I had the ring, I rarely showed it off. I just liked knowing it was there. It made me feel a little more different, a little more individual. Perhaps my creating a new hole in myself into which I inserted a foreign object was inspired by a desire to forge an identity in a bland generic Caucasian culture. The piercing was almost like my own personal tribal rite. Whenever I saw pictures of women from other cultures who had stretched, scarred, or otherwise altered their body, I wondered why they would endure such pain and discomfort for the sake of beauty or tradition. At the same time, a part of me envied their looped earlobes or elongated necks, because their distinguishing features served as symbols of their identities, differentiating them from the rest of the world but connecting them to their tribe.

There was no great revelation that preceded the removal of my ring. One day, I just looked down at it, and realized that piercing my navel had been a rather hollow gesture, and it no longer signified anything to me. At that moment, I realized I know who I am, I am proud of myself, I am a unique human being, and I decided I didn't need to mutilate myself with a piece of stainless steel to prove my individuality to myself or anyone else. Having a bellybutton ring no longer gave me a feeling of satisfaction. In fact, it actually made me feel somewhat pathetic for ever getting it in the first place, so I found some pliers and took it out then and there. Standing in my bathroom that day holding the freshly extricated ring on my palm, I felt empowered, free from the need to prove I could be a nonconformist, which I had often expressed by dyeing my hair unnatural colors like fuschia and turquoise. I realized that my struggle to be different was just as pointless as some

Essays

of my peers' constant worrying about being "normal" and fitting in, a desire which I'd often scoffed at. The opinion that matters most to me is my own. I'm not perfect, but I'm me, and I'm going to accept myself the way I am, and try not to waste any more of my life comparing myself to those around me.

Who knows, maybe I will dye my hair again if I find a beautiful color, because I like having brightly hued hair. Maybe in the future I'll get a tattoo. But the next time I make a major change to my body, it will be because I want it and because it makes me happy, and those will be the only reasons. I know that I will never submit my body to someone who doesn't care about me, drugs or excessive alcohol, or dieting to model myself after media-driven images of thinness. I might never have perfect thighs, but really, who cares? My value as a human being remains the same. Instead of focusing so much energy on my appearance, I'm going to invest my time in becoming a better person. I have the power to accomplish just about anything I set my mind to. Within myself, I have the resources to change the world. Today, I'm glad I had the experience gaining then losing that small hole in my navel, because it made me realize I am whole, just the way I am.

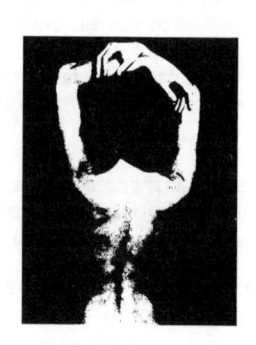

Voices of young women

13 to 15

Art

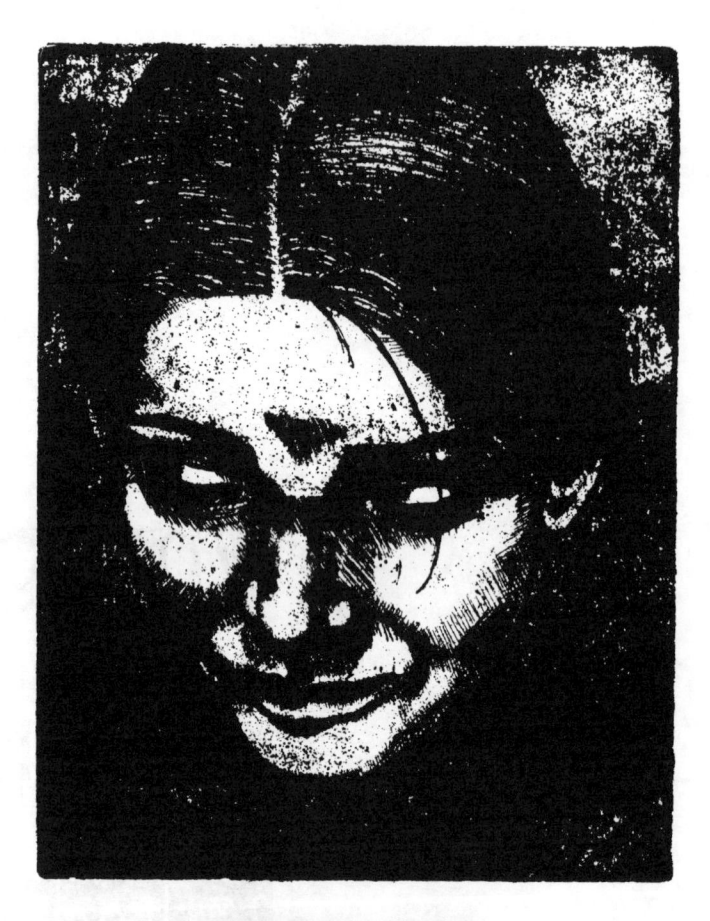

by Kasia Sowka

Untitled

Winning Essay

THE DANCE

by Charmaine McCraw

It was a beautiful summer day and the wind was nice, warm, and balmy. This was the day I was about to experience a feeling of a life time.

Myself and my aunts were on our way to a native gathering otherwise known as a pow-wow. The area in which we were headed for was a remarkably small place, a pinery. The tree stands and lake were so divine I could just fall down and let the sound of the wind going through the pines waft me away. The arbor was a little area in which many dancers in full regalia danced hard and proud. As we pulled up to the grounds, the sounds of the drums began to enter my heart. This feeling was an exceedingly honourable feeling, a feeling that only each individual could feel. The drums were alive, you could hear every single beat as if it were the beating of your heart. I commenced dressing and doing up my hair in the traditional french braids. As I put my regalia on a sudden feeling came through me. It was like an overwhelming feeling of joy. As I began to braid my hair I knew that this was the beginning to a wonderful day. I knew this because usually my hair is unco-operative when I begin to braid. Today, fortunately it went as if it were an intertwining rope, born to braid.

After all the hustle and bustle of getting ready to go into grand entry the moment came. It was the moment when, all of the sudden, my body just took off. The drums ran through my body and the energy was flowing. Each time I caressed the ground with my feet I rose higher. Soon I felt an exhilaration that I had never felt before. It felt as if I were going to touch the sky. The faster the drums went the faster and harder I danced. Although my muscles were telling me they were sore I guess it was my soul that would not let them stop. Then, at the last beat of the drum, I stopped. I stood there for awhile wondering what had gone through me. I was confused yet overwhelmingly happy. As people rushed by me to go and acquire a refreshing cool drink I remained in the same spot. My aunt Debbie came up behind me and broke me out of my trance. She asked if I was okay then, I finally knew what was going on. I had experienced the first opening to what my body could actually do.

I went to where my aunts and I were sitting and remained standing. I couldn't sit down I was too delighted with what I, and my body, had done. Later on the drums began again. I had the rush that I had had when I reached the top earlier. I began to dance as if I were a bird. My shawl glided through the air as if they were wings of the great eagle. My arms were the guide of my graceful shawl as they twirled and flew, a smile grew upon my face. My legs were like springs each and every time I met the ground I would spring up, and up, and up. Finally I reached the top. My body had actually done what it was meant to do and I was happy with what I had done. I was amazed at the work and spirituality my body had reached.

Winning Essay

The night went on and as the evening approached my aunts had a surprise for me. It was just after supper break, the traditional feast, and I heard someone calling my name. It was my aunt Ivy calling. I went over to where she was standing and she asked me if I would do her the honour of wearing her dress in the evening Grand Entry. I stood there shocked. I was not quite sure what I was thinking. I accepted her offering and began to dress in the new and honourable jingle dress.

Just as I had completed dressing the drums began to sound. This time as I entered the circle I went in as if I had grown in a way that nobody else ever had. Although the jingle dress is quite heavy, each step I took it felt like I was a feather just floating around in the summer breeze. At last, it was bound to happen, the eagle whistle called. As I heard the high-pitched sound of the whistle my body seemed to kick into overdrive. I danced harder and harder yet it felt like I was barely even touching the ground. The whistle blew four times and then another whistle blew, I danced and danced, I felt like I could dance all night. Then after all the dancing was done I remained in the arbor area for a while. I could still hear the drums and the sacred eagle whistle and even though I was not actually dancing I could feel my body content and performing, I did not want to leave.

Before that night I never knew what my body could do. I thought it was well just average. I'm telling everyone right now, I never knew what I could do until I just didn't think about it. I am proud of myself and of my body and what I can do and I hope all the girls gain the confidence that they need to be proud and stay strong.

Essays

DEADLY BATTLES
by Becca Digout

I was okay. At least I thought I was. Then all of a sudden my life came crashing down on me like ten thousand stabbing knives.

I feel so alone and empty inside that I need to cry out to prove to myself that I haven't used up all of my emotions. I need someone to hold me and love me. I'm sick of individuals telling me that maybe I will get better and they wish for me to soon be happy. Please don't wish my life away! Why is my life so out of control? Why? No one deserves to live like this, not even me. Especially when I don't know what I did to deserve this bottomless existence.

Thinking back two years I remember the night my mother walked in on me as I was vomiting after a large binge. I insisted that I was just feeling sick, denying any sign of an eating disorder. However, she didn't believe me and when my father returned home from work they both firmly insisted I had bulimia, a self destructive behavior that includes many different forms of purging your body of ingested foods. Pressuring me for the truth I broke down and cried so hard it hurt as I admitted that I had secretly been bulimic for over three months. I explained that I needed to be perfect so everybody would love me. By being as thin as a small child I could receive the unconditional love and care I once had at a younger age.

My parents quickly took action. They made arrangements for me to be hospitalized because of my drastic weight loss. I was forced to talk daily with a therapist and after one month of pretending, I fooled the professionals into discharging me. From that day on, my life became a vicious cycle as I was in and out of hospital. As my weight fluctuated I gave up hope completely and took up cutting myself as a coping mechanism. As long as I felt pain on the outside, I didn't have to deal with the confusing emotions inside.

Classified as suicidal, I decided to go to the extremes. As soon as the next crisis arrived, I overdosed on over the counter drugs. Even after having my stomach pumped and a brief hospital admission, I hadn't learned. Overdosing became my new way to deal with my feelings. I had lost a family member to cancer and faced a difficult breakup with a boyfriend. I couldn't show how angry and betrayed I felt, so I turned my feelings inside. I thought I had to solve everyone's problems and take on the world's grief.

About a month before Christmas 1997, I decided to take the offered help. I chose to stay in a treatment center until I could live safely at home. I was so fed up with my

Essays

living patterns that I was determined to conquer this living nightmare for good this time. I swallowed my pride and accepted the fact that I was emotionally ill.

Spending endless hours discussing my difficulties and listening to realistic feedback wasn't as hard as I had surely expected. The hardest part was coming to realize that I had feelings of my own. I wasn't supposed to hide my real feelings or try and take on the world's grief. I learned that perfectionism isn't worth all the internal scars. I also became well informed that it is impossible to properly help others if you are amongst your own difficult issues. It is important to help others in a beneficial way only when you yourself are well taken care of. As someone who likes to assist others, this news was both difficult and reassuring. However, once I got over the obstacle part of the situation, I was well on my way down the road to recovery.

I discovered that if I didn't want to feel happy then I wouldn't. Facing decision making and taking risks occur daily. I know that I can choose to be positive and I can choose to feel happy. Feeling happy would mean I would be doing something good for myself. Was I really ready to do that? I decided to take the risk. Taking that step was the best thing I could have ever done. I will give myself credit for that! Of course there are going to be days when I'm going to want to look in the mirror and criticize my body or say something negative regarding what I see, but I know in order to fully recover I will have to think more positively. So instead, I will compliment myself on at least one thing that I like. There has got to be something!! That's why when I look back on that journal entry I wrote on how alone and unloved I felt, I realize my mistake. I realize that those things are my responsibility. I need to be my own best friend. I must love myself before anyone else truly can.

Now that I am in the recovery process, I would be more than happy to try and help others. Even if this message only reaches out to one person, I can say I've made a difference. If you are hurting inside or you feel alone, don't deny it or try to cover it up. Talk to someone and keep talking until someone hears you or better yet, will listen to you. Tell yourself you want help and you want to feel happy and in time you will. Don't give up on yourself and don't do something that you will regret, because let me tell you sadly that the majority of people who attempt suicide and succeed would have regretted it given more time and thought. Don't make that same mistake, no matter how hard it is sometimes for you to believe in yourself. Life is a mixture of sunshine and rain. Focus on the sunshine!!! You will become the best person you can be. Other people will learn to accept you once you accept yourself. Once you stop judging yourself, you will have more time to love yourself. As with happiness - as you experience it, life will become more meaningful. Try it! It really does work. You deserve it!!!!

Art

by Elise Critoph

Friends

Essays

"DYING TO BE FREE"
by Erin Dowling

Well, if anyone's knocked on death's door, I rang the bell.

It all started for me five years ago, when I was ten years old, I was a really beautiful kid. I was 5 ft. 3" and I had gorgeous hair and a great figure. I was at the top of all my classes, and I had everything going for me. Then, I started to worry about my weight and appearance. I started to cut out the junk food and eventually it began to develop into a very serious issue. My wonderful parents would spend literally hours at a time trying to tell me that I was never, and was never ever going to be, fat. I wanted to believe them so bad, but something just wouldn't let me. That was only the beginning.

I started to worry about my weight in August of '93. By that December, my parents were so worried about me and I was so out of control, they didn't know what to do.

I had a serious obsessive compulsive disorder and am still struggling with it at times. I would make myself do everything in sets of threes or multiple of threes because those were my "skinny" and "magic" numbers. Somehow, I thought these numbers would change me. I would make separate trips for everything for putting one shoe on the shelf at a time, to never carrying two things in my hands at once, always going back for things - one at a time. I would always squat when I had to bend down, just to be different. I would wash my hands whenever I touched something. I would even limit myself to how many times I was allowed to go the bathroom. It was getting pretty ridiculous.

I would always tell people what I ate and always ask them what they ate. I would repeat over and over in my head what I had eaten that day. I would spend so much time studying and memorizing the labels on all the food packages in our house. I was always counting every single tenth of a gram of fat that I ate. I even had a belt that I would wear and make it smaller and smaller every day.

In late December of '93, my parents took me to a child and adolescent physician in Winnipeg, Manitoba, about an hour and a half drive from my home. He said I had a serious case of Anorexia Nervosa. I weighed 74 pounds. He was going to send me to the Children's Hospital in Winnipeg, but decided to let me go home on the condition that I drink high-calorie milkshakes, plus three meals a day, and spend each day with one of my parents. So, I temporarily quit school, grade six, and my mom temporarily quit her job as Registered Nurse.

I had to drink these shakes until about April of '94 which was when I could return back to school. That summer, after continuing to drink the shakes, I reached my "goal

Essays

weight" of around 100 pounds. I really got scared when I found out I had almost gained all of that weight back and I went into serious depression. I was so afraid of being fat that I lost weight again. In two weeks I ate nothing, lost about 11 pounds, terrified my parents, and was admitted to the Children's Hospital in Winnipeg.

To make a long story short, after about two and a half months, they got my weight back up, though I was not eating any food, only Ensure meal replacements. They discharged me in November of '94. I was no less afraid than when I had been admitted. In fact I was more determined than ever to live my life as the worst anorexic.

I began seeing a psychiatrist in Brandon, Manitoba. A five hour return trip every week, and I was also seeing my family doctor.

By March of 95, I had gone back down to about 75 pounds and was admitted to hospital in a neighboring town. There, I continued to control and manipulate everyone and everything I did so that I could lose more weight. It worked. Anorexics are very clever. They have so many tricks up their sleeves. They find so many ways to hide food, get rid of food, exercise, deceive, things you wouldn't even believe were possible.

They decided not to weigh me like they had every day at the Children's Hospital. It got to the point where I was so terrified of food that I had to be spoon fed. Even then, the nurses and aides had to force me. I was eventually tube fed. That's when they stick a tube down your nose that goes into your stomach and they feed you through it. I had this three separate times in the nine months that I was there. The first time, it was in for three or four months, the second time was about one month and the third was really a bunch of times, because I kept making the nurses nuts by always pulling it out when they weren't around. The first time I pulled it out, I felt like I was ripping my insides apart. I was in so much pain, but I just didn't care anymore. I was the patient from hell. You name it, I did it. From throwing food at nurses, to screaming and swearing, to knocking over tables, to nobody gave up on me. The nurses were really wonderful and my doctor was really amazing, too. Though I made their lives hell, I always knew they cared about me. I had my own nurse each day. I was finally discharged November 30th of '95.

I was home on the condition that I maintained my caloric intake and all my meals had to be supervised. Each week I met with a dietitian, the psychiatrist in Brandon and a local therapist. I went back to school and was home for a little over a year.

September of '96 I was still doing okay, so I started high-school with my friends.

By December of '96, we were really having trouble. Every single meal was fighting and torture. I was really abusive and manipulative and still had a depression problem. All I wanted to do was lose more weight. I was still determined to live my life as a slave to my anorexia. I looked like death.

Essays

In January of '97, "Friends of Erin" was formed in my town to raise money for me to go and live with a therapist in Winnipeg. Many people contributed to give me a chance to live. To them I will always be grateful.

When I got there, things didn't start to get better right away. In fact, things got a lot worse. I continued to lose weight. The lowest I remember weighing myself was 47 pounds and I still wanted to lose more. I got to the point where I couldn't even walk properly because I had no muscle left in my legs. I couldn't make it to my room up on the third floor without nearly passing out. I didn't breathe properly and my heart would even skip a beat once in a while. I was so tired and could hardly keep my eyes open. I was so cold all the time and my therapist had to come and check on me every night to make sure I hadn't stopped breathing. Every night before I went to sleep, I would write to all the people I loved because I didn't know if I'd wake up the next morning.

If it weren't for this wonderful woman, I don't know where I would be today. She helped me to love myself again and helped me WANT to get better. She showed me the path, but it was up to me to walk it. I finally realized this and started to turn things around. By October of '97, I came home to stay and things have been going really well. I love life now and am trying to live it to the very fullest. I know I am not 100% cured, but each day I get closer.

It has been a dark, lonely, and frightening road. I know that without the love, prayers, and care of my family, friends, doctor, therapists, nurses, and others involved in my life I would not have had the courage to fight my way back to freedom.

A song that gave me strength and hope was "Hero" by Mariah Carey.

"So when you feel like hope is gone
Look inside you and be strong
And you'll finally see the truth
That a hero lies in you."

If you are reading this and you know you are trapped in this darkness, there is help for you. You can be free, reclaim your life, and be happy again. I know because I've been to the bottom and am climbing to the light. I've come a long way and now I love doing things to take care of myself instead of destroy myself.

Even though I am only 15, I would like to write a book and get it published. I also think that as a career, I'd like to set up some sort of an in-house clinic for girls with eating disorders. Nobody should have to go through all this pain and suffering alone and I want to dedicate my life to helping other girls like myself.

Thank-you for listening to my story.

Art

Sagara Yaigueré

Self-Portrait

Essays

MY STRUGGLE AND GLORY
by Yenny Espinal

As a teenager I've suffered through many things, just to look like the cover model on the newest issue of some teenage magazine. I've tried to look like society's "perfect image". I've tried dieting, exercising and even starving myself. This is my story of a struggle I suffered even before becoming a teenager.

When I was ten my body started changing, I began to look different from the other girls. I had breasts and all the other girls didn't, I also had big hips. I was not happy with my body and I felt like an outsider. I weighed about 115 lbs and the rest of the girls weighed 80 lbs or so. From then on I began to get concerned I thought I was some "mutant" or something.

The summer of 1993, I went to my country, El Salvador, to visit some family there, and I got terribly sick. It was unexplainable. I thought I had gotten sick because it was a different environment from what I was use to. After I came back to Canada, I again was feeling ill. I was taken to the doctor and all he said was that they were symptoms of menstruation and that I was going to go through it soon.

My parents and I left it at that. The doctor gave me some vitamins but they didn't help. I once again got sick in December. I was barely eating and barely paying attention in class. I could not eat. I tried to but it would just come up again. I would sometimes faint and not be able to get up. My body lost calcium and iron and almost destroyed my kidneys. I was feeling great pain in my uterus but didn't tell my mom about that much. Sometimes I couldn't sleep because the pain was too intense.

Then Christmas 1993 came and I was taken to Sick Children's Hospital. I spent my Christmas Eve there. The doctors had found out what was wrong with me: I had begun to menstruate but all the blood was accumulated in my uterus. They told me they had to operate.

They operated on me on New Year's, and I had to stay in the hospital for two days. They weighed me. I only weighed 85 lbs. I knew this wasn't a case of anorexia or bulimia but it sure felt like it was both.

After I left the hospital I was better, I was some how happy. I weighed 85 lbs, I knew I shouldn't have been but the sad truth was that I was relieved about that. From then I decided to maintain this weight although I knew I had to make some sacrifices. And so I began starving myself. I only ate once a day and drank a lot of water. I began to exercise and join school teams. I wanted to be thin. Who would have thought that a girl who was almost eleven thought about her image and how thin she was, but I was not like any other girls, I wanted to grow up too quickly.

Essays

My starving went on from the time I was ten to the time I became thirteen. It wasn't something I did excessively. I would go off and on. I would sometimes stuff myself and then starve for a straight week. It was a circle of starving and not starving. My starvation caused many problems in my family. I was cranky most of the time and I got into many fights with my parents. I no longer cared about school, image was everything for me. It was about being thin and staying thin.

My parents weren't aware of what I was doing. They thought that I was just going through a stage or something. Little did they know that I was drowning in a pool of devastation. My friends didn't even know what I was going through I hid it so well, but I was bottling it up inside my system. I no longer had self-esteem, I was so alone in my depression without a soul to guide me.

I became so involved in myself that I no longer went out with my friends or family. All I wanted to do was stay at home and work out every last bit of energy that I had. I was lucky enough that my friends kept talking to me because I was a real witch to them. I began seeing the counselor at my school I started to talk to her about my problems but I never really told her about my starving. Later she found out, she told me that a teacher had noticed that I was not eating during lunch. I began to get angry and didn't know where that teacher got off worrying about me, for goodness sake I wasn't even her child and could do whatever I wanted. I denied everything but the counselor saw right through me, she knew I had been starving myself. She informed my parents about it and they were a bit surprised because they never thought something like that could have happened to their daughter. I felt so horrible my mother was crying like it was her fault.

The next summer I realized that I was not doing a healthy thing and that I was just making my body worse. I began to eat properly and exercise. I no longer worry about my weight because I like myself for who I am inside. I despise magazines that just show a pretty a face. How about a pretty personality or how about brains? Now I only look at real role models — women who make a change without a worry about their image. One day, I hope to become a journalist and make a change in society. Let young women know the truth of things and that the best thing to do is to be themselves.

I've learnt a great deal through my experience. I've learnt to be strong. Hopefully teenage girls could read this and be aware that they could fall victims of society's so-called "image". Every being is beautiful even if it's a different size, shape, or colour. We are beautiful to our parents why can't we be beautiful to the world? I now follow the rule, "Love thy neighbour as you love yourself." For I consider the whole world beautiful.

I've matured and that is what people do when they go through difficult times. Maybe girls can mature without living in corruption of self image. Maybe we together can make a difference and tell each other, "WE ARE ALL BEAUTIFUL!!!"

Essays

No Title

by Lindsay Friis

Ever since I was a little girl, I can remember playing with Barbie, imagining what it would be like to have clothes like her, hair like her, and long legs like her. I thought she was beautiful. I was never a really chubby kid, but I was also not a waif. I figured that when I grew up I would be beautiful and thin, like Barbie. I was expecting that to come when I became a teenager. I was a pre-teen who liked to read teen magazines with the latest fashion trends and make-up tips. Those magazines were full of incredibly mature looking teens with "great" figures. It was when I turned about ten that I began to feel fat and ugly. This essay is not about me being anorexic or bulimic. It's just about a young girl who battles to feel confident about herself, and more specifically, her weight. I didn't have any reason or any outward signs of an eating disorder. I just felt inside that I needed to lose weight. I wasn't sluggish or indolent, I even participated in many sports. Until I was eleven I loved to figure skate. I quit and began to justify my actions by saying I was too fat to wear spandex anyway. I had my little plans, my own little diet plans when I was about twelve. Of course, at that age I definitely didn't have the capacity to do that.

It was in grade seven then that I began cutting health information out of magazines, exercising, eating like a bird in front of peers, and hoping to get thin. When that didn't come, I began to get mad at myself, and criticized my thin friends, telling them they needed to put on some weight. I had low self esteem, although I tried to hide that with an aggressive and extroverted personality I wasn't tortured by anyone about being overweight. It was me that felt I was fat, and the only person who could change that was me. I realized that, but I still strove to be thin. I'd skip meals, usually lunch, and sometimes even breakfast. Not for any particular reason, just that I thought less food and more exercise meant less fat. That was not a smart thing to think. I ended up binging sometimes and eating a lot and lazing in front of the TV. I put on a lot of weight in grade seven.

The next year was a little better, I refined my style to become somewhat sporty, which was more preferential. A new group of friends helped me focus on the better things, saying over and over again, "You have a cute face, who cares if you're a little chubby? It's cute!" While that helped at the time, it made me think worse things about my stomach, hips and thighs. I was, and still am, a pretty good student, making first class, or silver honors every term. I was well recognized for that. In grade eight, I was in student government, and I was the co-editor of our yearbook. It may sound egotistical, but what I wanted was for the boys to say I was pretty and the girls to not like me because they thought I was pretty too. But that didn't come, and I felt irrational to think it ever would. I dreaded summer because of the revealing clothes that go along with it. My thin friends would get guys looking at them all the time. They swore that were looking at me too, but I knew they weren't. I would try to take it

Essays

gracefully but inside it hurt a lot. I really wanted to have a thin body, I very, very badly desired that.

    Now, I'm fourteen. True I still have a very long time until I am grown up, but I believe that I have apprehended what it really means to be beautiful. I have found that no matter your weight, or any other physical characteristic for that matter, you are a beautiful person. This year I have begun exercising, not to get thin, but to be healthy In realizing that you don't have to be thin to be beautiful, I have become a much happier person, who is a lot more fun to be around. I am hoping my story will help people realize that it is not just girls with eating disorders that have an unhealthy body image, and a hard time dealing with their weight. I also hope my story will help girls, younger or older, realize that it's o.k. not to be waif-thin, and that you alone have to be the one to accept your body, or nobody else will.

    Lately there has been more and more reflections on a healthy body image in society. More and more magazines, like Chatelaine, have published articles which I believed have helped me a great deal. Plus size models, especially Emme, have proved that no matter how thin or big you are, makes no difference to just how beautiful you can be. It seems most models are incredibly thin and sick-looking. It also seems when Hollywood talks about the sexy, pretty women of show biz, the women are coincidentally a duplicate of the perfect Pamela Lee body image. Hollywood is coming along though, by breaking the super-star mold with healthy, muscular actors like Kate Winslet, Minnie Driver and Demi Moore. I think society, although we still have a long way to go, is finally learning about the impact a certain body image has on people, especially young girls. Any one type of body image is not healthy for anyone. There are an immeasurable number of body types, all beautiful. The world will soon realize that.

Art

by Sarah Walker

Ink nude

Essays

LATE DEVELOPER
by Alison Louder

When I was a little girl, developing didn't seem like such a big deal to me or to any of my other friends. We saw it as something that only Mommy did (and sex was just a game that our parents played). In fourth grade it was newly interpreted as gross. But then, in fifth grade, young girls got a whole new perspective about it. Some of my friends had already developed small breasts and had just gotten their periods. A few complained about how horrible it was for hours on end, others couldn't wait to get theirs and the rest just simply didn't care. I was one of those who didn't care all that much. By the time I was twelve, I had some small breast buds of my own which, over the course of sixth grade, came to look like two little triangles stuck to my chest. That wasn't much, considering I was the only sixth grade girl in my class who still didn't have her period or any honest to goodness breasts. I dyed my hair auburn red that year. The only times it ever got on my nerves was when boys would make fun of me for it, but they stopped towards the end of the school year. That summer went great and I was excited about starting high school.

The big day came and I went off to school wearing a loose, Indian patterned shirt over my camisole. I didn't know anyone there, so no one spoke to me. As I looked at the other girls of my age, I realized that ***all*** of them had both bigger breasts and hips than me. They all wore makeup, cool nail polish, and had nice hairstyles, whereas I didn't wear any of those. Heck, they all wore brassieres while I only needed silly little sports bras. That's when I realized that I was a late developer. I immediately felt shy and ashamed of myself. The only thing some of them had that I didn't were crooked teeth, since I'd gotten mine fixed the year before. But my shyness soon faded away when I made friends –boys and girls– who liked me for who I was, and I became my old wacky self again. Once before a swimming class, a new friend of mine asked me "You're going in? With your period?" I simply told her that I didn't have mine yet. A few girls gawked and told me how lucky I was not to have it. Still, I wasn't so sure. It's one thing not having your period. It's another thing not having your period or breasts or big hips. A few weeks later, I had started wearing lip gloss and changed my hair from long, reddish buff-length braids –which had earned me names like Anne, Caddie Woodlawn and Pippie– to a loose shoulder-length cut. The rest of the year went by great, and I slowly continued to develop. I turned thirteen and was officially the most undeveloped teenage girl in my class (*in* my mind, that is). But I grew big enough for a brassiere. Come summer, another dilemma approached.

My little sister by 20 months started to develop as well, and soon her breasts were bigger than mine. For me, that was the biggest crisis in my life. How could my Rebecca be more developed than me? I was older, I had to come first! While these thoughts kept racing on a track in my head, her chest grew bigger and she even made a point of

Essays

flaunting it in front of my guy friends. Some people thought she was older than me. I was disgusted by her attitude, so disgusted that I began to get jealous. So I decided to talk to my mother about it. Her most helpful reply was "Well you two are only 20 months apart, that's not a big difference. Besides people grow at different rates." DUH! I kind of knew all that. It shocked me to realize that my own mother didn't even understand what I was going through.

When we went on our trip to Atlantic Canada, all went well, even though the jealousy I felt for my sister was no longer a mystery to me. Then, in St John's, Newfoundland, our Uncle decided to take us to one of the town's many museums. While we were there, Rebecca had to use the washroom and wanted me to come with her. So I waited outside her stall, blabbing to her about something when she suddenly said: "Al, I got my period!" My first reaction was "Yeah, right. Nice try!" but when she told me it was all over her under wear, I suddenly thought "Oh my God, it can't be!" I ran to tell my mom and she let me go get a "just in case" maxi from the car for Rebecca. That very day, my jealousy increased about 800 per cent.

Just before starting eighth grade, I started wearing real makeup, jewelry and nail polish. I styled my now golden hair in many different ways and wore cool clothing. I had discovered how good I was with hair and cosmetics, unlike Rebecca who always wore the same hairstyle and who never did her makeup quite right. When I went back to school, my friends saw me as "the new and improved Alison" although they soon became accustomed to my new look. I liked the way I looked, partly because it made me look older.

Now, it's towards the end of eighth grade and ***I still*** don't have my period. I'm still waiting for the big day to come. But now, it doesn't matter anymore. I've gone back to the old "I don't care about periods" stage. Sure, some people bug me about it but I just laugh it off. The funny thing is that I'm the envy of every girl in my class who has her period, and Rebecca doesn't seem to be enjoying hers one bit.

Essays

THE ULTIMATE CONNECTION
by Jennifer MacDonald

To me, my body and its image has always been a mystery. I think as I grow older, and encounter more of these 'adolescent experiences', that once very small mystery becomes a large novel.

Throughout my years, my body has constantly endured rough, hard concrete and asphalt, tight uncomfortable running shoes, wet and slippery hills, and mud-filled ditches. Although cross-country running might not exactly seem glamorous, to me it is one of the most exhilarating experiences that one can possibly imagine. It is hard to explain, but the adrenaline you feel when running and finishing is incomprehensive.

On several occasions, my body has overcome many pitfalls and hardships, that have definitely surprised me, such as when I was required to swim 400 m at the Scarborough Swim Meet, when I was only used to swimming a constant 50 m. Or when running in two feet of snow and -5oC degree weather, at this year's Ontario Cross Country Championships. Or maybe it was even when I practiced for a whole year, and our school entered the Toronto Marathon. All of these events played an important role in my self esteem today. They contributed to my overall acceptance level, by helping me realize that I can overcome even the most difficult tasks, but first I must try.

When I think of trying times, one particular incident comes to mind. Last year, when I first entered grade nine, I was mentally pumped and ready to take on any leap that faced me. I began training, the March before the September season started, in hopes to qualify for the Ontario Finals Secondary Athletic Association (OFSAA '96), in Toronto, Canada.

As the season progressed, and each new meet passed, I became better prepared by the day. Still, in the back of my head, was that ultimate achievement of the Ontario Finals.

By the time the Scarborough Finals rolled around, I was almost in top physical condition, which earned me a second place. They only accepted three runners to represent Scarborough in the Ontario's, and luckily I was one of them. From now on in was to be the most grueling test of my physical endurance. My daily routine consisted of about an hour of constant running, with a combination of hills and flat lands.

The race was scheduled for Saturday, and on Thursday evening, I decided to go for a light twenty minute jog, to loosen up. I don't usually like to run the day before the race, so I was prepared to take Friday off. As I was running down a fairly steep hill, I slowly began to round the corner near the bottom of the decline. It was November, so my mind was mainly focused on finishing the cold route, more than anything.

Essays

The road was fairly uneven, and in a blink of an unwatchful eye, I had gone over on my ankle, badly injuring it I started to hobble home as tears of failure streamed down my cheeks. I could not face the fact that this incident might stop me from competing in the Ontario's. Then in blind arrogance towards my body, I started to continue running, bracing the incredulous pain. This action only harmed my ankle more than anything.

My heart had been broken, which hurt more than the constant pain in my ankle. The person who inspired my hope was my mom. She when she drove me right off to the chiropractor's office, who stayed for an extra two hours to tend to my ankle.

Friday was one of the worst and toughest days. I made two separate trips to the doctor's, and had to ice my ankle most of the day. This day involved tough emotional strain. I had to search deep within myself, and to try to contemplate; could all that I had built up for, possibly be relinquished in this one moment?

By the time Saturday rolled around, my ankle was still in a great deal of pain; but if it were not for those caring people around me, I might not have run in the race. My stride was off, and the thick tensor bandage slowed me down, but I tell you, when I finished that race, I felt more proud than if I had come in first.

It taught me not to sweat the small stuff; and to treat my body as a tool which could accomplish anything that I put my mind to. It has made me mentally stronger, and aware that our bodies are precious instruments that must be looked after constantly. I think that this is the most important lesson. Teenage girls now, automatically believe that they can not do it, based on their previous lifetime experiences. If they would only have the courage to believe in themselves, and give whatever it might be a chance, maybe some day, they can shoot for the stars. I now always remember, that there is no harm in trying.

This season, as I crossed the finish line at the Ontario Finals 1997, a warm feeling came to heart, as I recalled the great connection that I had made with my body, just a year before.

Art

> You'll never tell.
> And nobody will believe me.
> We'll just call it our little secret.
> Shall we?
> As you rape me.
> And I let you.

by Jenn Smith

Our little secret

Essays

IT'S MY BODY
by Ashley Portielje

My mom always says, "Our body is the temple that houses the spirit within us, and that her temple needs some major renovations." She also compares her body to our ninety year old home and says her basement is cracking and her floors are crooked. My mom has a great sense of humour! She was diagnosed with polio at the age of four. Since then, she has had 18 operations, and now suffers with chronic pain, but that doesn't stop her.

My mom is a great model for me. Even though she has a disability and wears a brace on her leg, she tries to do everything an able bodied person would do. She swims, stretches and works out in a gym. As well, she is very conscious and strict about nutrition in our home. She reminds me of an Energizer Bunny, who keeps going and going and going.

As a result of this upbringing, I too, am concerned with taking proper care of my body through a good diet and exercise. However, this doesn't mean I don't eat ice cream, chips or cookies!! I'm not perfect, nor do I want to be! I do care about how I look but I don't want to spend my life staring in the mirror. I'd much rather play and participate in my favourite sports – basketball, volleyball, swimming and skiing.

For as long as I can remember I have been encouraged to look beyond the body and to see and enjoy the person for who they are and not what they look like. In other words, don't judge a book by its cover. Although this is a wonderful philosophy to live by, it's not always possible for me to be unaffected by the images of young, thin, pretty girls in magazines.

Sometimes I think I've gained a bit of weight and something just doesn't look right or I don't like my hair. This is because I get caught in the trap of comparing myself to models. Even other people I went to school with a couple of years ago criticized my body. They told me I was too tall and called me chicken legs, spider legs and even giraffe legs. The boys called me flat chested. I hated these comments because they were so hurtful I felt like a loser.

Now at age fifteen in grade nine, I step back and say to myself, "Hey, ya' know what? I love my body. And I love it because I know where everything is, all my little freckles, all my tiny hairs. It's just comforting to know. And on top of it all, it works, all the little parts and all the big parts. It does exactly as it's told."

My body didn't always listen to me. At birth my doctor discovered that I had Congenital Hip Dysplasia. Moments after my birth I was whisked away from my mother, and was immediately wrapped into a cast stretching from my brand new belly button to my tiny ankles, in a spread eagle position. I wore this for three weeks. Mom said it was

Essays

very uncomfortable for a new baby, and I cried a lot. It was extremely difficult to comfort, cuddle and breast feed a stiff baby. I couldn't fit in the conventional car seat so my parents put me in a huge wicker basket and strapped me and the basket to the back seat of the car.

At the end of these weeks I was then put in a harness for seven months. My mom thought my body was prematurely well developed because I was able to sit upright at such an early age. She later found out, after I fell over, that it was the harness supporting me! I was fortunate that the doctor found the problem at birth, otherwise, like my mom, I would have experienced several operations during childhood and into adolescence, perhaps even into adulthood. I would not be the active teenager that I am now. So I am very thankful to have an able body.

I think my early childhood experience and watching my mother has influenced me and the way I look at life, and how precious my life is. Through my childhood, I had to go to specialists at the Toronto and Ottawa Sick Children's Hospitals quite frequently to make sure my hips were growing properly. I still go for check-ups even today, but not as frequently as in the past. At these hospitals I see children my age and younger in wheelchairs, casts, crutches, braces and so on. I remember thinking at a young age, how lucky I was to know that I would not suffer permanent damage because it was caught in time. I still feel very fortunate.

I think people should focus more on how lucky they are to have a fully functional body, one that they can walk with, run with and love with. There will always be people that are not so fortunate. Personally, I don't think that we should be preoccupied with flabby thighs, spongy buttocks and small breasts. If your body works, take care of it. Feed it good food. Exercise it. Play with it. It's the only body that you're going to get so accept it and LOVE IT!

When I walk around my high school I don't see these Seventeen girls, the sad emaciated models who look like people you want to take home and feed. I see girls of all shapes and sizes, a picture of the real world. In my opinion, the media should start showing these girls. The focus should not be on beauty and diet. How many times do you see these words on the cover of magazines? People should concentrate on being healthy, both on the inside and the outside. Find out what people are doing with their lives as a whole, not just exclusively focusing on the body. This would make the magazines far more interesting. Not only would it help young girls, like me, accept themselves for who they are, but it would also raise our self-esteem.

So, in my family, I not only take good care of myself by staying healthy and fit but I equally take care of my inner spirit. I frequently must remind myself though, of what really matters, because I can sometimes become influenced by media images, in spite of what I say. But then I look at my mom and I know that at least I can walk to the corner store without any pain. So, what is really important?

Essays

ARMADILLO

by Emma Ziolkowska

There were footsteps piercing my abdomen. I guessed The Children were sporting high heels for the occasion. Or perhaps they just had nails sticking out of their sneakers. I concluded the latter, because what are the chances of The Children wearing high heels in a stomach? It's not very probable.

They hung onto the insides of me, digging their tiny hands deeper, clinging. One of them lost its grip, struggled in vain, then fell, a scream echoing after her. I am not that deep, so she fortunately didn't get wounded. But, being Children, once one of them expressed pain, they all simultaneously felt it as well. They howled in unison. The chorus line begged me to let them out, (I hadn't even been aware that I had let them in) while the backup singers cooed "Pleeaasse!!!" For extra emphasis on their cause, they dug their nail clad feet into me even farther.

My eyelids fluttered open, my pupils widening immensely. I was curled in a ball; an armadillo seeking its own protection. My comforter was twisted around my legs, gnarled and confining. I unwound myself and tumbled out of bed. The pain shot through me like a bolt of electricity, singeing everything in its path. This stomach ache was unknown to me. I could not recall the feeling of it from the time before. I was more frightened than anything else, and being half asleep, my logic was not at its full potential.

My sister was the closest thing that could help me. I shook her and she grumbled something, covering her eyes with her arm. Tears were streaming down my face, burning my skin. The Children were becoming angrier.

"Sarah," I whimpered, and clawed at her shoulder blades.

She turned to face me abruptly, her hair disheveled, a pillow crease across her cheek. Her lips tried to form a word, and she croaked out, "What?"

"There are people crawling in my stomach" I sobbed, "It hurts. Make them go away." I guess she didn't register what I said, because she merely dismissed it and told me I had the flu. Then she retreated to the other side of the bed and fell asleep. I rushed into the bathroom.

I must have been in that eggshell room for hours. The cold linoleum sturdied my shaking legs, and the white lights cleared my head. Everything came into sharp focus, the countertop gleaming, the mirror reflecting an anguished 12 year old.

Essays

Weak and weary I returned to my bed. The people were still there, but they must have been tired as well because I was only vaguely aware of their presence.

I slept and dreamt of white rooms and derelicts.

That stomach ache has haunted me for the past two years. It has returned often, sometimes 10 times in a week, other times not for months. As I grew used to the sensation that I was going to be sick, I realized that if I occupied myself with something intriguing it would momentarily go away. If I paid attention to the pain mounting inside of me it only got worse.

After the first few months of these occasional spasms my mom took me to our family doctor. He probed me with his cold fingers, asking me to identify the area of irritation. When I explained my symptoms, he put me on a lactose intolerant diet.

This failed.

My mother also suffered from stomach problems, and when we had lived in Alberta she had gone to see an allergy specialist. She returned home with swollen arms and a booklet full of foods she was allergic to.

Despite her precautions and careful planning, she still got sick.

So when we moved to Ontario, my mom took us to yet another specialist. My only allergy is willow trees. (Which happens to be my favourite tree.) My mom's results were a tenth of her previous ones.

I then remembered a book I had read by Judy Blume when I was younger. It was called *Then Again, Maybe I Won't*. It was about a teenage boy who suffered from anxiety attacks, which caused him to have stomach aches. They were similar to my own.

In a magazine I saw an advertisement to calm nerves. It said it was prescribed for people with Nervous Stomach Disorder. I finally had a name.

As time passed, I learned to deal with the pains and how to fend off disaster. I felt I had some control over the situation, although I really didn't. My stomach aches controlled me.

When I get stressed out, I don't relieve myself of the stress well. So, the anxiety builds up and builds up, gaining momentum until I can't contain it. This is when I get sick.

The point of the stomach ache is to relieve anxiety, but it only causes me more. I get so worried about pretending I feel fine when I am out that I do get sick. It's like a broken merry-go-round and I'm a fake plastic horse.

Essays

I have often considered going on medication to ease the pain. But my family and my friends have convinced me not to. They don't want me to become dependent on chemicals. Really, I wouldn't mind having something else take the burden.

I have tried to explain my stomach problem to friends before, but they usually conclude that I am weak because I can't deal with my own life.

They don't see that I am coping, and very well. I just do it in a different way.

In fact, I am not weak and pathetic, I am strong. I have learned that I can defeat anything that happens. If I am able to conquer the hurricanes inside of me, why can't I triumph over the mere thunderstorms of everyday?

Conclusion

CONCLUSION...OF SORTS

These essays... wow! These are the best of 600 essays about body image by young women aged 13-19 from across Canada. You name it, these young women have an opinion and a personal experience with it, ranging from:

- Depression and anxiety attacks
- Eating disorders
- Developing breasts, shopping for a first bra
- Body hair: To shave or not to shave
- Body piercing, tattoos, hair dyes, driving Mom insane
- Dancing, including belly-dancing
- Physical as well as mental self-torture
- Controlling your body as a way of controlling your life
- The ecstasy of sport, building up muscle, being strong
- Dealing with unwanted touching
- Exciting discovery of the body's secret places
- Impact of sexual experimentation on self-esteem
- Living with disabilities
- Exploring cultural traditions related to the body
- Feeling ugly, feeling beautiful, feeling whole
- Gaining confidence and self-awareness

The perspectives in these essays are as varied as the young women themselves. Some view their growing breasts as a horror ("goose-bumped pendulums of fat"), others as a wondrous delight. One speaks of the pros and cons of being the last one in her class to develop. Some are anxious about change, others welcome it. Some view their body as an enemy, others as a beautiful sculpture, and some as a friend with whom to go dancing, running, camping, biking, canoeing, swimming and mountain-climbing.

One disturbing fact is that we received more essays about anorexia and bulimia than any other body image topic. This happens when, as one writer describes it, one's "sugary expectations" of growing Baywatch boobs and looking like "Cindy, Shalom, Pamela, Naomi, Elle, Linda, Bridgit, Amber" turn into the "vinegar reality" of having an ordinary, imperfect body. They describe in horrifying detail the many effects of eating disorders, including growing "the body hair of an orangutan." At sixteen, one young woman overcoming an eating disorder says, "I still look more like a gardening utensil than a woman."

> "I would not change my body to anyone else's, even a model. Every scar and wrinkle on my body represents moments of my life."
> - Candice Jwaszko

Conclusion

Never before have young women been given so many unrealistic body images to live up to: Today's magazine pictures are not only airbrushed, they are digitally remastered. Products and services such as laser hair removal, dangerous weight-loss pills, breast implants, plastic surgery, new and improved make-up, cellulite creams, liposuction, promise that you can look digitally remastered too. Well...guess what.

These young writers speak of the calorie-reducing tricks of feeding your dinner to the dog, turning up your stereo so your mother can't hear you vomit, viewing chocolate as a threat. One young woman pretends she is wearing blue lipstick because at 5 foot 4 and 78 pounds, her lips really are blue from the cold which envelops her bony body. Some blame the media, like Much and YM. Others speak of high expectations of parents, or the standard-setting "bored middle-aged men and the women that stand by them and don't correct them." Some blame the teasing of peers and boys at school, friends who think Baby Spice is too fat and should be renamed "Pudgy Spice". Ultimately, they blame and punish themselves.

Many of the writers who have been through horrifying stuff have retained a great sense of humour, which has probably helped them survive. One describes her interesting perspective on her mother's best friend who worships a fat goddess, and talks about Scary Spice grabbing Prince Charles' butt. One dreams of winning an Academy Award and thanking her dog on national television. One got away from societal expectations in a fabulous camping trip with girlfriends in which they became wild women in the forest, gleefully ignoring all rules of fashion.

> "I will climb mountains with this body."
> - Emily Bodenberg

> "When you're thirteen and just getting used to the changing world around you, the last thing you need is the constant reminder of what you are not, and what you and hundreds of others wish they could be but most likely will never become."
> - Denise Fuller

One young woman speaks of leaving a controlling boyfriend, and another about the men and boys she knows going gaga over silicone-enhanced young women in the media. We expected more about relationships with young men, but there were far more about the relationship with the self, parents, friends, Clairol and pink disposable razors! The message: Body image is more about what's in your mind than what's in the mirror. It's more about your relationship with yourself than with potential love-interests.

Parents and teachers may not appreciate all of these stories, as we did not screen out those whose views do not conform to what is considered good and acceptable for young women. One essay, for example, is about how the writer's tattoo, obtained against her mother's will, is a symbol of strength for her. These are young women's own words and thoughts. That is their power.

Conclusion

These body image essays deal with more than the physical transformations all young women experience, but the spiritual challenges of overcoming life-threatening eating disorders, sexual harassment, or intense depression and self-hatred. One young woman who comes a long way from being deathly ill to going back to school says, "All flesh is beautiful; this body is mine." Most of these essays are stories of hope, some arising from a long litany of pain. Many women twice their age have yet to learn the wisdom and insight these writers have to share.

> "My fingers paint a love story across my flesh and the image in the mirror slowly smiles."
> - Gillian Burrell

The afterword in this book is a feminist analysis of what the young women have said. So I prefer in this conclusion to let the clarity, simplicity and common sense of the writers themselves act as a challenge to regimented thinking of all kinds - from the consumerism and materialism that make women miserable for the sake of cosmetics profits, to the labelling of women as helpless victims of a "capitalist, patriarchal" plot, which does not give women credit for our own strength, and absolves us of any responsibility for our own lives. Yes, we must deal with circumstances that try to box us into certain behaviours and ways of life. But inside of us, we have the power, the strength, the courage and the gumption first to change our own lives and then to change the world. Before most of the young women in this book were even able to drink legally or vote, they dealt with and discovered what spiritual leaders, self-help books, therapists and other well-wishers try to tell people of all ages. They figured it out. Let's listen to them for a change, instead of trying to tell them what their lives are about.

"I know people half my [dress] size, double my intellect, who still have not discovered the grey area that lies between beauty and ugliness. They've yet to realize that beauty isn't achieved through fashion or make-up. It isn't even achieved through the insult of others. Beauty can't be achieved in any form. It is possessed by all. It's just matter of uncovering it."
-Cheryl Amanda Gullage
16-19 year-old category

"I have learned to love my body as it is: because it is beautiful, because it is healthy, because it is mine. I have learned that confidence shows through in your eyes and your stride, and people respond to it more strongly than anything else in your appearance."
- Sarah Jasper
16-19 year-old category

Well said.

Marika Morris, Research Coordinator
CRIAW

Afterword

Afterword

What is there to add, following these wonderful essays? What more can be said after such eloquent writing? Not much needs to be said and here I can only reiterate what these young women have poignantly related.

The young women tell their stories with passion and great lucidity. Their writings are articulate and enlightening. Most importantly, the young women who contribute to this anthology do understand and name power relations. They aptly describe and analyse the webs of power which shape their everyday lives and which in turn, they alter by their everyday actions.

Reading these stories is a humbling experience for an older woman/feminist. The young women here are not passive. They are not mere victims nor do they need patronizing or moralizing tales from an older generation. If many of the young women we read have suffered and experienced self-hatred through the body, they have also recovered and found their path and own self-loving voice, vision and touch. They can teach a lesson or two to other young women and to many older women suffering from hatred of the flesh in contemporary western society.

The young women are well aware that the body is a social construct, that while each body is unique, bodies are also literally shaped and marked by specific cultures and histories. The body as a cultural production indeed lies at the intersection of the personal and the social. The body speaks of social divisions and status as well as personal preferences and aspirations. As the young women express so well, the body is both created by the collectivity and is the creator of individual identity.

The body is a crucial site of the production of gender categories in contemporary western society. Moreover, structures of oppression such as patriarchy (or masculinism), white supremacy, agism, class oppression and heterosexism all articulate and establish themselves through the body. The investigation of bodily practices therefore provides a window into the study of larger social relations (Beausoleil 1992, 1994, 1996, 1998).

Contemporary western society is not only patriarchal or masculinist but also a profoundly dualistic society where body and mind are conceptualized as separate and unequal realms. Mind (or reason) has primacy over bodily (and emotional matters). Women are associated with the domain of the body while men are seen as masters in the area of mind/reason, this ideology justifying the oppression of women and the appropriation of their bodies (Spelman 1982). In a patriarchal or masculinist context, women suffer numerous constraints and controls through the body. Feminists have denounced this state of affairs, some suggesting that women transcend the body and reach the realm reserved to men (DeBeauvoir 1953), while others have questioned the very dichotomy between body and mind (Rich 1976; Spelman 1982).

Afterword

Yet other activists and researchers have underlined that women are never completely subjugated in a patriarchal and dualistic order, that they are, in fact, at the same time both objects and subjects. Recent feminist scholarship in particular has emphasized the struggles, negotiations, coping strategies, and even subversion and rebellion which women have demonstrated in the area of the body (Young 1990; Smith 1990; Davis 1995; Fisher and Davis, ed. 1994; hooks 1993).

The stories in this book show the tensions young women experience as they are both object and subject in and of their culture. They document the struggles and strategies young women develop, alone and with others, in a society which devalues and diminishes them, literally, through their bodies.

The pain in these stories has a lot to do with norms of femininity about body shape. The obligation/obsession of thinness and the oppression of fatness are fundamental features of the current standards of femininity in western society. Many stories describe women's tortured relation to food and their attempts to diet and even starve themselves. The narratives therefore show a continuum of pain, from unhealthy eating to medically diagnosed eating disorders. In a feminist perspective, it is crucial to understand, as some young women underline, that all these practices are linked to the social production of femininity and the oppression of women (King, 1994; Brown and Jasper, eds, 1994). The stories also document the danger of overexercising and the tyranny of mirrors, linked to a tortured relation to food and distorted perceptions of the body. Moreover, they denounce unrealistic, unattainable and damaging ideal images of beauty and femininity in mass media and overall popular culture. In addition, interactions with others are at times sources of concern, pain and self doubt (Nichter and Vuckovic 1994). The transition to adolescent femininity and womanhood may also be a source of pain. While many girls long to become women, puberty and associated bodily changes sometimes bring disappointments and suffering. The sexualization of these transitions may also cause feelings of confusion and inadequacy. Young women are thrust, inexperienced, into a (hetero)sexual world in which they are viewed as, and expected to be, sex objects. Young women are also torn between conforming to standards of adolescence and femininity and their desire to achieve individuality (Hudson 1984; McRobbie 1991, 1994).

But the stories in this anthology are not only about pain, tensions and disappointments. They also document joy and self love through the body. Some stories are strikingly moving celebrations of the body as a source of sensuality, athletic accomplishment, spirituality, and as a wonderful expression and vessel of art and creativity. Through their stories, these young women show they experience the body as a fundamental connection to one's feelings and to the world. Some young women explicitly say they achieve unity of body and mind, of feelings and intellect, of sensuality and reason. Some powerfully describe how they have learned to live well with illness, disability or injury. Many young women tell tales of friendships and love of

Afterword

family as crucial to their well being and overall sense of health. Thus, these stories bear witness to the importance of affection, support and friendship in coming to terms and learning to love one's body.

In sum, the texts relate both the joy and pain young women experience through the body in contemporary western culture. They provide insights into the norms of femininity and its subversion. The young women themselves clearly recognize and sharply analyse political forces at work in the production of femininity. Taken together, these texts fruitfully explore the dynamics of oppression and resistance, of self-fulfilment and self-destruction, and of love, friendship and loneliness. Thus, these stories document the complexity and multifaceted nature of women's relations to the body.

Ultimately the narratives in this anthology are stories of recovery and learning to love oneself. They show young women's search for and achievement of higher self-esteem, freedom and independence. In one word, the stories here bear witness to young women's empowerment. Moreover, these young women want to help others and to take part in social change. Using vivid and beautiful language the young women who have participated in this anthology show that writing is healing and that documenting and sharing their road to recovery is crucial to self love as well as to helping others.

Natalie Beausoleil,
Professor of Sociology
University of Ottawa

Afterword

REFERENCES

Beausoleil, Natalie. 1992. *Appearance work: women's everyday makeup practices*, Ph.D. diss., Department of Sociology, University of California, Los Angeles.

Beausoleil, Natalie. 1994. Makeup in everyday life: an inquiry into the practices of urban American women of diverse backgrounds. *Many mirrors : body image and social relations*, N. Sault (ed.). New Brunswick, NJ: Rutgers University Press.

Beausoleil, Natalie. 1996. Parler de 'soi' et des 'autres' femmes minoritaires : problèmes rattachés aux catégories d'identité dans la recherche féministe. *Femmes francophones et pluralisme en milieu minoritaire*, Dyane Adam (ed.). Ottawa: Les Presses de l'Université d'Ottawa.

Beausoleil, Natalie. 1998. Corps, santé, apparence et vieillissement dans les énoncés de femmes francophones en Ontario. *Reflets* 4(1) Spring.

Brown, Catrina and Karin Jasper, eds. 1993. *Consuming passions: feminist approaches to weight preoccupation and eating disorders*. Toronto: Second Story Press.

Davis, Kathy. 1995. *Reshaping the Female Body: The Dilemma of Cosmetic Surgery*. New York: Routledge.

De Beauvoir, Simone. 1953. *The Second Sex*. Translated by H.M. Parshley. Harmondsworth: Penguin..

Fisher, Sue and Kathy Davis, eds. 1993. *Negotiating at the margins: the gendered discourses of power and resistance*. New Brunswick, NJ: Rutgers University Press.

Hooks, bell. 1993. *Sisters of the Yam: black women and self-recovery*. Toronto: Between the Lines.

Hudson, Barbara. 1984. Femininity and adolescence. *Gender and generation*, A. McRobbie et M. Nava (eds). London: Macmillan.

King, Dixie L. 1994. Food, Sex, and Salvation: The Role of Discourse in a Recovery Program of Eating Disorders. *Many Mirrors: body image and social relations*, N. Sault (ed.). New Brunswick, NJ: Rutgers.

Mc Robbie, Angela. 1991. Jackie and Just Seventeen: girls, comics and magazines in the 1980s. *Feminism and youth culture*. Boston: Unwin Hyman.

Mc Robbie, Angela. 1994. Shut up and dance: youth culture and changing modes of femininity. *Postmodernism and popular culture*. London, New York: Routledge.

Afterword

Nichter, Mimi and Nancy Vuckovic. 1994. Fat talk: body image among adolescent girls. *Many Mirrors: body image and social relations*, N. Sault (ed). New Brunswick, NJ: Rutgers.

Rich, Adrienne. 1976. *Of woman born*. New York: Norton.

Smith, Dorothy E. 1990. Femininity as Discourse. *Texts, Facts, and Femininity*. New York: Routledge.

Spelman, Elizabeth V. 1982. Woman as body: ancient and contemporary views. *Feminist Studies*, 8 (1) 107-131.

Young, Iris Marion. 1990. *Throwing like a girl and other essays in feminist philosophy and social theory*. Indianapolis: Indiana University Press.

Resources

Community, National and International Resources

The purpose of this list is for us to help YOU find the resources you need. It is a guide to selected organizations and networks across Canada and beyond. If you need help finding other resources and information, CONTACT US!

Veuillez communiquer avec nous si vous désirez de l'information en français. Vous trouverez une section française de ressources dans le livre: *Le corps en tête: les jeunes femmes se prononcent*, publié par l'ICREF en octobre 1999, sous la direction de Sara Torres.

The Editing Team.
email. criaw@sympatico.ca
website. http://www3.sympatico.ca/criaw

COMMUNITY RESOURCES

KIDS HELP PHONE
1-800-668-6868
http://kidshelp.sympatico.ca

24 hour anonymous counselling and referral service for youth 5-20 years old. Caller may request either a man or woman counsellor.

LOCAL HOSPITAL / CLINIC
Emergency departments in most major centres have staff on-call (counsellors/psychologists) who can deal with emergencies involving eating disorders.

LOCAL WOMEN'S CENTRE
Telephone number in white pages.

A wealth of information and community resources and referrals available on a wide variety of topics. Women of any age are welcome.

PUBLIC HEALTH UNIT
Telephone number in blue section of white pages.

Focus on health promotion through positive lifestyles. Clinics are most often staffed by female doctors and nurses. Referrals available. Call ahead for information.

YOUTH ORGANIZATIONS

THE CANADIAN ABILITIES FOUNDATION

489 College Street, #501, Toronto, ON M6G 1A5
www.enablelink.org

The Canadian Abilities Foundation (CAF) has as its mission to provide Information, Inspiration, and Opportunity to People with Disabilities (of all ages), their friends, families and the professionals who work in their service. CAF publishes *Abilities Magazine* and maintains *EnableLink*, an online service.

CANADIAN YOUTH FOUNDATION

215 Cooper Street, 3rd Floor, Ottawa, ON K2P 0G2
tel. 613 231-6474, fax. 613 231-6497
web site: www.cyf.ca

The Canadian Youth Foundation has published a directory of youth organizations located across Canada.

NAC YOUNG WOMYN

NAC Young Womyn (affiliated with the National Action Committee on the Status of Women) is a group of diverse, active young womyn who are taking charge and making change to better society for young womyn.

Contact Denise Campbell, the Young Feminist Vice-President at (416) 932-1718 or denise@tgmag.ca.

NETWORKING YOUTH NATIONALLY/ ALLIANCE NATIONALE DES JEUNES

www.nyn.on.ca

This web site contains an on-line database (free of charge) which operates as a resource directory and an information clearinghouse for youth groups / organizations across Canada.

POWER CAMP

PO Box 20282, Ottawa, ON K1N 1A3, tel. 613 562-9629, tel. 613 562-2291
e-mail: powercmp@storm.ca
website: www.powercamp.on.ca

Power Camp is a community development project based in Ottawa designed to address issues specific to young women related to poverty, racism, body image, violence against women, the environment, health, education, creativity and activism!

THE STUDENTS COMMISSION

website: www.tgmag.ca
email: tgmag@tgmag.ca

NATIONAL OFFICE	ST. JOHN'S OFFICE	BUREAU DE MONTRÉAL	VANCOUVER OFFICE
70 University Ave.	PO Box # 23046	1671 boul. Henri-Bourassa	Est.1367 West Broadway,
Suite 1060	Churchill Square	Bureau 1	Suite 321
Toronto, ON	St. John's, NFLD	Montréal, QC	Vancouver, BC V6H 4A9
tel. 416 597-8297	tel. 709 737-3139	tel. 514 382-1401	tel. 604 730-8170
fax. 416 597-0661	tel. 709 737-2437	tel. 514 382-3474	fax. 604 738-7175

The Students Commission is a diverse, global-minded organization that is run by youth for youth across Canada. It strives to create opportunities for empowerment through innovative and educational processes and products. The Students Commission has developed a unique, youth-driven, conference format that enables young people to turn their ideas into action.

YOUTH NET / RÉSEAU ADO

401 Smyth Rd., Ottawa, Ontario K1H 8L1
tel: (613) 738-3915, 738-3914 fax: (613) 737-3917
website: www.youthnet.on.ca
e-mail: kodsi@cheo.on.ca

Youth Net/Réseau Ado (YN/RN) is a bilingual youth mental health promotion and mental illness prevention program run by youth for youth. The essence of their community-based programmes is to respond to the needs of youth as they identify them. YN/RN reaches out to the experts - youth- via focus groups and asks them what issues effect their lives. They are also beginning to provide long-term clinical support groups. Currently, YN/RN offers programmes in Eastern Ontario and Western Quebec, however, they are in the process of developing satellite centres across the country. YN/RN also publishes a monthly newsletter called Youth Fax. It is written and edited by youth for youth in an informative and artistic manner on all sorts of youth issues. So far, two issues of the newsletter have discussed body image.

DIRECTORIES OF YOUTH ORGANIZATIONS ACROSS CANADA

Available from:

CANADIAN YOUTH FOUNDATION
215 Cooper Street, 3rd Floor
Ottawa, Ontario K2P 0G2
tel. 613 231-6474 fax. 613 231-6497
website: www.cyf.ca

**NETWORKING YOUTH NATIONALLY/
ALLIANCE NATIONALE DES JEUNES**
www.nyn.on.ca

BODY WISE WEB SITES

Canadian Resources

CHATELAINE MAGAZINE'S GUIDE FOR PARENTS AND TEACHERS ON TALKING TO GIRLS ABOUT BODY IMAGE

www.chatelaine.com/read/health/ptguide.html

MEDIA WATCH

517 Wellington Street W., Suite 204, Toronto, ON M5V 1G1
tel. 416 408-2065   fax. 416 408-2069
email. mediawatch@myna.com
www.mediawatch.ca

International Resources

ABOUT - FACE

www.about-face.org

This web site "combats negative and distorted images of women."
The site includes a recommended reading list which is divided into the following sections: Feminist/Critical Analyses of Eating Disorders/ Body Image; Case Herstories: examples of women's struggles with body image and eating disorders; Acceptance of Body Size; Adolescent Girls: Their development experiences regarding body image, sexuality and other topics; and a list of related books available through Amazon Press. The Recommended Reading list can be found at:
www.about-face.org/resources/books/index.html

GO GIRLS

"Giving girls inspiration and resources for lasting self-esteem"

www.goldinc.com/gogirls

HOW SEVENTEEN UNDERMINES YOUNG WOMEN

www.igc/org/fair/extra/best-of-extra/seventeen.html

JUST SPORTS FOR WOMEN

www.justwomen.com

LARGESSE :THE NETWORK FOR SIZE ESTEEM

www.fatso.com/fatgirl/largesse

SIZE WISE

www.sizewise.com

WEBZINES

Girl Zone Webzine **www.girlzone.com** includes a free e-mail service

Go Girl Webzine **www.gogirlmag.com** Webzine "girl power"

gURL, an on-line magazine **www.tsoa.nyu.edu/gurl**

Hues Webzine **http://hues.net** multi-cultural webzine by and for young women.

Reluctant Hero **http://reluctanthero.ets.net**

Teen Voices **www.teenvoices.com**

MAGAZINES

Canadian

Reluctant Hero. By Girls for Girls, Publisher and Editor-In-Chief: Sharlene Azam, Editor: Shelia Heti, Toronto.

International

HUES: Hear Us Emerging As Sisters, New Moon Publishing: Duluth, Minnesota.

> HUES is hip, smart, and down-to-earth. A woman's guide to power and attitude, HUES promotes self-esteem and self-sufficiency among young women, ages 16-30, of different cultures, sizes, and lifestyles. Published bimonthly.

Teen Voices. Boston, Massachusetts Women Express, Inc.

> Teen Voices is an interactive magazine that challenges media images of girls and women. Published by a multicultural collaborative of teens and young women, it offers an intelligent alternative to glitzy, gossipy, fashion-oriented publications that exploit the insecurities of their young audiences. It honours young women's potential as leaders, empowering them to create a better world. Ages 12-19.

CLINICS, ASSOCIATIONS AND WEB SITES THAT SPECIALIZE IN EATING DISORDERS

Canadian Resources

ANOREXIA NERVOSA AND BULIMIA ASSOCIATION (ANAB).

3640 Wells Avenue, Windsor, ON M5C 1T9. tel. 519 253-7421, fax. 519 253-7545
Web site www.ams.queensu.ca/anab/sistes.htm.

Associated with Queen's University, this web site lists a number of recommended international sites and books on eating disorders.

RESOURCES

AWARE (ACTION ON WOMEN'S ADDICTIONS - RESEARCH - EDUCATION)
PO Box 86, Kingston, ON K7L 4V6. tel. 613 545-0117, fax. 613 545-1508
email. aware@Kosone.com

BRITISH COLUMBIA EATING DISORDERS ASSOCIATION
841 Fairfield Rd., Victoria, BC V8V 3B6, tel. 250 383-2755, fax 250 383-5518
email www.bceda@islandnet.com

BRITISH COLUMBIA EATING DISORDER RESOURCE CENTRE
St. Paul's Hospital, 1081 Burrad St., Vancouver, BC V62 1Y6.
tel. 604 613-5313, toll free. 1 800 665-1822 fax. 604 631-546
email edrcbc@direct.ca

NATIONAL EATING DISORDERS INFORMATION CENTRE
Toronto General Hospital College Wing, 200 Elizabeth St., Rm. 2-332, Toronto, ON M5G 2C4
Tel. 416 340-4156
www.nedic.on.ca

SHEENA'S PLACE (HOSPICE FOR EATING DISORDERS)
87 Spadina Rd., Toronto, ON M5R 2T1. tel. 416 927-8900, toll free.
1 888 743-3627, fax. 416 927-8844

WOMEN'S HEALTH CLINIC
Third Floor, 419 Graham Ave., Winnipeg, MB R3C 0M3. tel. 204 947-1517,
voice mail. 204 947-2422
fax. 204 943-3844 TTY. 204 956-0385

International Resources

AMERICAN ANOREXIA AND BULIMIA ASSOCIATION (AABA)
www.aabainc.org

ANOREXIA NERVOSA AND RELATED EATING DISORDERS (ANRED)
www.anred.com

EATING DISORDERS AWARENESS & PREVENTION INC.
www.edcp.org

EATING DISORDERS REVIEW
www.gurze.com/edr.htm

This is a site for clinicians and is published by Joel Yager, MD (University of New Mexico, Alberquerque). It features summaries of research from journals and unpublished studies.

INTERNATIONAL JOURNAL OF EATING DISORDERS
webmd.lycos.com/topic_summary_article/DMK_ARTICLE_40031

OTHER CLINICS, ASSOCIATIONS AND WEB SITES OF INTEREST

CANADIAN DIETETIC ASSOCIATION

480 University Avenue, Suite 601, Toronto, ON M5G 1V2.
tel. 416 596-0857, fax. 416 596-0603

CANADIAN INSTITUTE OF CHILD HEALTH

885 Meadowlands Drive East, Suite 512, Ottawa, ON K2C 3N2
tel. 613 224-4144
website www.cich.ca

CANADIAN WOMEN'S HEALTH NETWORK

203-419 Graham Avenue, Winnipeg, Manitoba R3C 0M3
tel. 204 989-5500
Clearinghouse Toll Free Line. 1 888 878-9172
fax. 204 989-2355
email. cwhn@cwhn.ca

A SELECTED LIST OF NATIONAL CANADIAN WOMEN'S ORGANIZATIONS

ABORIGINAL WOMEN'S NETWORK

316-181 Higgins Ave., Winnipeg, MB, R3B 3J1
tel. 204 942-2711

AFRICAN WOMEN RESOURCE AND INFORMATION CENTRE

#712, 602 Whiteside Place, Toronto, ON M5A 1Y8
tel. 416 214-4823

CANADIAN ASSOCIATION FOR THE ADVANCEMENT OF WOMEN & SPORT AND PHYSICAL ACTIVITY (CAAWS)

308A, 1600 James Naismith Drive, Gloucester ON K1B 5N4
tel. 613 748-5793
e-mail. caaws@caaws.ca
website. www.caaws.ca

ASSOCIATION CANADIENNE DES FEMMES ARABES

#2, 2435, ch Lucerne, Montréal, QC H3R 2K5
tel. 514 733-0481

ASSOCIATION DES FEMMES AUTOCHTONES DU QUÉBEC

503-460 rue St. Catherine ouest, Montréal, QC H3B 1A7
tel. 514 954-9991

RESOURCES

CANADIAN ASSOCIATION OF SEXUAL ASSAULT CENTRES

77 East 20th Avenue, Vancouver, BC, V5V 1L7
tel. 604 872-8212

COLLECTIF DES FEMMES IMMIGRANTES AU QUÉBEC

7124, rue Boyer, Montréal, QC H2S 2J8
tel. 514 279-4246

CONGRESS OF BLACK WOMEN OF CANADA

590 Jarvis Street, Toronto, ON M4Y 2J4
tel. 416 961-2427

DISABLED WOMEN'S NETWORK (DAWN)

PO Box 22003, Downtown PO, Brandon, MB R7A 6Y9
tel. 204 726-1406   fax. 204 726-1409
e-mail. dawnca@canada.com

EQUALITY FOR GAYS AND LESBIANS EVERYWHERE (EGALE)

177 Nepean Street, Suite 306, Ottawa, ON K2P 0B4
tel. 613 230-1043

IMMIGRANT AND VISIBLE MINORITY WOMEN AGAINST ABUSE (IVMAA)

PO Box 67041, Ottawa, ON, K2A 0E0
tel. 613 729-3145

NATIONAL ACTION COMMITTEE ON THE STATUS OF WOMEN (NAC)

234 Eglinton Ave East, Suite 203, Toronto, ON M4P 1K5
tel. 416 932-1718   fax. 416-932-0646
email. nac@web.net

NATIVE WOMEN'S ASSOCIATION OF CANADA

9 Melrose Avenue, Ottawa, ON K1Y 1T8
tel. 613 722-3033

PAUKTUUTIT INUIT WOMEN'S ASSOCIATION

192 Bank Street, Ottawa, ON K2P 1W8
tel. 613 238-3977

WOMEN'S HEALTH IN WOMEN'S HANDS

2 Carleton Street, Suite 500, Toronto, ON M5B 1J3
tel. 416 593-7655   fax. 416-593-5867
e-mail: whiwh@web.net

Selected Bibliography

The following bibliography provides a selection of material available on a variety of subjects of interest related to young women and body image. It is divided into the following categories: Health and Body Image; Eating Disorders; Beauty, Glamour and Culture; Sports, Fitness and the Outdoors; Women with Disabilities and; Being a Teenager. These categories are further divided into Canadian and international sources. The bibliography contains a variety of material ranging from books geared towards young women, academic articles, and resources of interest to parents and teachers including films, videos and educational packages. While this list is certainly not exhaustive, it is intended to be used as a starting point to help you in your search for information on body image.

HEALTH AND BODY IMAGE

Canadian Sources

Cole, Susan G. 1996. "The Body Politic Goes To The Mall." *Herizons*. 10 (3): 43.

Correia, Fatima and Niva Piran. 1994. "Self Help: Maintaining The Status Quo." *Canadian Woman Studies /Les cahiers de la femme*. 14 (3): 87-91.

Crook, Marion. 1991. *The Body Image Trap: Understanding and Rejecting Body Image Myths*. Vancouver: Self-Counsel.

Daymond, K. "Bodies on the Line." *GLQ: A Journal of Lesbian and Gay Studies*. 4 (1): 59-65.

Friedman, Sandra Susan. 1997. *When Girls Feel Fat*. Toronto: HarperCollins Canada, Ltd.

Hirschmann, Jane and Carol Munter. 1997. *Women Stop Hating Their Bodies: Freeing Yourself From Food and Weight Problems*. Toronto: Fawcett Book Group.

Poulton, Terry. 1997. *No Fat Chicks: How Big Business Profits Making Women Hate Their Bodies - How To Fight Back*. Toronto: Birch Lane Press.

Poulton, Terry. 1996. *No Fat Chicks: How Women Are Brainwashed To Hate Their Bodies And Spend Their Money*. Toronto: Key Porter Books.

Rice, Carla. 1994. "Out From Under Occupation: Transforming Our Relationships with Our Bodies." *Canadian Woman Studies/Les cahiers de la femme*. 14 (3): 44-51.

Rivard, Lise. 1993. "Apres l'inceste: troubles de l'alimentation: nouvelles questions." *Femmes d'action*. 22 (4): 35-36.

International Sources

Bordo, Susan. 1995. *Unbearable Weight: Feminism, Western Culture and The Body*. Berkeley: University of California Press.

Bordo, Susan. 1990. "Reading the Slender Body." Evelyn Fox Keler and Sally Shuttleworth (eds.) *Body/Politics: Women and the Discourses of Science*. New York: Routledge, 83 - 112.

Brumberg, Joan Jacobs. 1997. *Our Girls: Growing Up In A Female Body: An Intimate History*. New York: Random House.

Douglas, Carol Ann and Liz Quinn. 1995. "Girlspeak: Empowering Girls." *Off Our Backs*. 25 (11): 6-7.

Douglas, Susan. 1995. *Where The Girls Are: Growing Up Female in the Mass Media*. New York: Time Books.

Eagle, Carol J. 1994. *All That She Can Be: Helping Your Daughter Maintain Her Self –Esteem*. Distican, Inc.

Edut, Ophria and Rebecca Walker (eds.) 1998. *Adios Barbie: Young Women Write About Body Image And Identity*. Seattle: Seal Press Feminist Publishing.

Grogan, Sarah and Nicola Wainwright. 1996. "Growing Up in the Culture of Slenderness: Girls' Experiences of Body Dissatisfaction." *Women's Studies International Forum*. 19 (6): 665-673.

Hesse-Biber, Sharlene. 1996. *Am I Thin Enough Yet?: The Cult of Thinness and The Commercialization of Identity*. London: Oxford University Press.

Manore, Melinda M. 1996. "Chronic Dieting In Active Women: What Are The Health Consequences?" *Women's Health Issues*. 6 (60): 332-341.

Norton, Kevin et al. 1996. "Ken and Barbie At Life Size." *Sex Roles: A Journal of Research*. 34 (3-4): 287-94.

Peterson, Anne C. 1994. "Psychological and Social Issues During Adolescence: Depression and Body Image Problems in Adolescence." *Women's Health Issues*. 4 (2): 63-65.

Pinkola Estes, Clarissa. 1997. *Women Who Run With The Wolves*. New York: Ballentine.

Sandford, Wendy. 1992. "Chapter 1: Body Image". The Boston Women's Health Collective (ed.) *The New Our Bodies, Ourselves*. New York: Simon and Schuster, 23-29.

Wolf, Naomi. 1998. *Promiscuities*. New York: Fawcett.

Wolf, Naomi. 1990. *The Beauty Myth*. London: Chatto & Windus Limited.

EATING DISORDERS

Canadian Sources

Brown, Catrina and Karin Jasper (eds.) 1993. *Consuming Passions: Feminist Approaches To Eating Disorders and Weight Preoccupation*. Toronto: Second Story Press.

Claude-Pierre, Peggy. 1999. *The Secret Language of Eating Disorders: How You Can Understand And Work To Cure Anorexia And Bulimia*. Toronto: Vintage Canada.

Claude-Pierre, Peggy. 1997. *The Secret Language of Eating Disorders*. Toronto: Random House of Canada, Ltd.

Dolan, Bridget and Inez Gitzinger. 1994. *Why Women? Gender Issues and Eating Disorders*. Toronto: Scholarly Book Services.

Eating Disorders in Athletes. Specialized Bibliography. Ottawa: Sport Information Resource Centre.

Langford, Jan. 1991. "Accepting Yourself Is The Key." *The Optimist*. 17 (4): 12.

Rice, Carol and Leslie Langdon. 1991. "Women's Struggles with Food and Weight as Survival Strategies." *Canadian Woman Studies /Les cahiers de la femme*. 2 (1): 30-33.

Rock, Melanie. 1992. "Guilty of Secret Surrenders to Abundance: Women, Binging and Purging." *Atlantis: A Women's Studies Journal/Revue d'etudes sur les femmes*. 18 (1-2): 217-26.

Sault, Nicole (ed.) 1994. *Many Mirrors: Body Image and Social Relations*. New Brunswick: Rutgers University Press.

International Sources

Andersson, Mia. 1995. "Mother-Daughter Connection: The Healing Force in the Treatment of Eating Disorders." *Journal of Feminist Family Therapy*. 6 (4): 3-19.

Berman, Nina. 1993. "Disappearing Acts: Interviews and Photographs [Women With Eating Disorders]." *Ms*. 3 (5): 38- 43.

Cooper, Peter J. 1995. *Bulimia Nervosa and Binge-Eating: A Guide to Recovery*. New York: New York University Press.

Costin, Carolyn. 1997. *Your Dieting Daughter: Is She Dying For Attention?* New York: Brunner/Mazel.

Fallon, Patricia et al. (eds.) 1994. *Feminist Perspectives on Eating Disorders*. New York: Guilford Press.

Frederick, Christina M and Virginia M. Grow. 1996. "A Mediational Model of Autonomy, Self-Esteem, and Eating Disordered Attitudes and Behaviors." *Psychology of Women Quarterly*. 20 (2): 217-228.

Harris, Linda et al. 1991. "Teen Females in Minnesota: A Portrait of Quiet Disturbance." *Women and Therapy*. 11 (3-4): 19-35.

Hesse-Biber, Sharlene. 1991. "Women, Weight and Eating Disorders: A Socio-Cultural and Political-Economic Analysis." *Women's Studies International Forum*. 14 (3): 173-191.

Heywood, Leslie. 1996. *Dedication to Hunger: The Anorexic Aesthetic In Modern Culture*. California: University of California.

Kuba, Sue A. and Diane J. Harris. 1994. "Ethnic Identity, Acculturation, and Eating Disorders in Women of Color." Paper presented to the *American Psychological Association*. Available from: California School of Professional Psychology, 1350 M. Street, Fresno, Ca 93721.

MacSween, Morag. 1993. *Anorexic Bodies: A Feminist and Sociological Perspective on Anorexia Nervosa*. London: Routledge.

McEvoy, Victoria. 1994. "How Many Calories In Half An M and M?" *Journal of the American Medical Women's Association*. 49 (2): 60-61.

Maine, Margo. 1991. *Father Hunger: Fathers, Daughters and Food*. Carlsbad, California: Gurze.

Malson, Helen M. 1997. *The Thin Woman: Feminism, Post-Structuralism, and the Social Psychology of Anorexia Nervosa*. London: Routledge.

Martz, Denise M et al. 1995. "The Relationship Between Feminine Gender Role Stress, Body Image, and Eating Disorders." *Psychology of Women Quarterly*. 19 (4): 493-508.

Newman, Leslea. 1991. *Somebody To Love: A Guide To Loving The Body You Have*. Third Side Press.

Olson, Mary E. 1995. "Conversation and Writing: A Collaborative Approach to Bulimia." *Journal of Feminist Family Therapy*. 6 (4): 21-44.

Robertson, Matra. 1992. *Starving in the Silences: An Exploration of Anorexia Nervosa*. New York: University Press.

Romney, Patricia. 1995. "The Struggle for Connection and Individuation in Anorexia and Bulimia." *Journal of Feminist Family Therapy*. 6 (4): 45-62.

Steiner-Adair, Catherine. 1991. "When the Body Speaks: Girls, Eating Disorders and Psychotherapy." *Women and Therapy*. 11 (3/4): 253-266.

Thayne, Emma Lou and Becky Thayne Markosian. 1992. *Hope and Recovery: A Mother-Daughter Story About Anorexia Nervosa, Bulimia, and Manic Depression*. Watts.

BEAUTY, GLAMOUR AND CULTURE

Canadian Sources

Budgeon, Shelly and Dawn Currie. 1995. "From Feminism To Postfeminism: Women's Liberation In Fashion Magazines." *Women's Studies International Forum*. 18 (2): 173-186.

Sproule, Margaret. 1998. "Hair: On The Razor's Edge." *Herizons*. 1 (2): 18-19.

International Sources

Brownmiller, Susan. 1984. *Femininity*. New York. Simon and Shuster.

Ducille, Ann. 1994. "Dyes and Dolls: Multicultural Barbie and the Merchandising of Difference." *Differences*. 6 (1): 46- 68.

Higginbotham, Anastasia. 1996. "Teen Mags: How To Get A Guy, Drop 20 Pounds, and Lose Your Self-Esteem." *Ms*. 6 (5): 84-87.

SPORTS, FITNESS AND THE OUTDOORS

Canadian Sources

Canadian Association for the Advancement of Women and Sport and Physical Activity, (CAAWS/ ACAFS). 1994. "Eating Disorders: There's Hope If Caught In Time." *Action*, 1.

Canadian Association for the Advancement of Women and Sport and Physical Activity, (CAAWS/ ACAFS). 1995. "Gymnastics, Figure Skating, Address Serious Issues." *Action*, 1.

Edwards, Peggy. 1993. *Self-Esteem, Sport and Physical Activity*. Ottawa: CAAWS/ ACAFS.

Lenskyj, Helen. 1995. "What's Sport Got To Do With It?" *Canadian Women Studies/Les cahiers de la femme*. 15 (4): 6- 10.

International Sources

Arnold, S. Copland. 1992. "Transforming Body Image Through Women's Wilderness Experiences." *Women and Therapy*. 15 (3/4): 43-54.

Cohen, Greta L. 1993. *Women in Sport: Issues and Controversies*. Thousand Oaks, California: Sage Publications, Inc.

Dubowsky, Hadar. 1993. "Identity Politics at Summer Camp: Here's Where I Learned to be a Jew and a Woman." *Lilith*. 18 (2): 20-25.

Jones, Wanda K. et al. 1998. "The Health Effects and Benefits of Physical Activity in Women." *Women's Health Issues*. 8 (2): 74-80.

Zimmerman, Jean and Gil Reavil. 1998. *Raising Our Athletic Daughters: How Sports Can Restore Self-Esteem and Save Girls' Lives*. New York: Doubleday.

WOMEN WITH DISABILITIES

Canadian Sources

Driedger, Diane and April D'Aubin. 1992. "Women With Disabilities Challenge the Body Beautiful." *Arch Type*. May- June.

Di Marco, L.C. 1996. "What Happened To Equality?" *Women's Education des femmes*. 12 (2): 6-10.

Jolivet, Colette. 1995. "Une identité autre: ou l'extreme visibilité." *Femmes d'action*. 24 (3): 16-19.

Kaufman, Miriam. 1995. *Easy For You To Say: Q's and A's for Teens Living with Chronic Illness or Disability*. Toronto: Key Porter Books Ltd.

Odette, Francine. 1994. "Body Beautiful/ Body Perfect: Challenging the Status Quo: Where Do Women With Disabilities Fit In?" *Canadian Woman Studies/ Les cahiers de la femme*. 14 (3): 41-43.

BEING A TEEN

Canadian Sources

Carlson, D. and H. Carlson. 1999. *Girls Are Equal Too: The Teenage Girl's How-to-Survive Book*. Toronto: Monarch Books of Canada.

Day, Dian. 1990. *Young Women In Nova Scotia: A Study of Attitudes, Behaviour and Aspirations*. Halifax: Nova Scotia Advisory Council on the Status of Women.

Folkers, G. and J. Engelmann. 1997. *Taking Charge of My Mind and Body: A Girl's Guide to Outsmarting Alcohol, Drug, Smoking, & Eating Problems*. Toronto: Monarch Books of Canada.

Johnston, Andrea. 1999. *Girls Speak Out: Finding Your True Self*. Toronto: Scholastic Canada Ltd.

Olmes, Janelle and Elaine Leslau. 1992. "Chapter 1: The World and the Self." *We're Here, Listen To Us!: A Survey of Young Women In Canada*. Ottawa: Canadian Advisory Council on the Status of Women.

Young Women Speak Out: 1992 Symposium Report. Ottawa: *Canadian Advisory Council on the Status of Women*, 1992.

International Sources

Abner, Allison and Linda Villarosa. 1996. *Finding Our Way: The Teen Girls' Survival Guide*. New York: Harperperennial Library.

Gray, M. and Samantha Phillips. 1998. *Real Girl, Real World: Tools for Finding Your True Self*. Seattle, Washington: Seal Press.

Schwager, Tina and Michele Schuerger. 1999. *Gutsy Girls: Young Women Who Dare*. Minneapolis, Minnesota: Free Spirit Publishing, Inc.

FILMS AND VIDEOS

Canadian Sources

Beating the Streets. Director: Lorna Thomas. National Film Board of Canada. 1998, 48 min. 3 sec.

Beauty Begins Inside Series. Three-part video collection, Savoury Productions with the National Film Board of Canada:

Beauty Begins Inside: Pressure Zone. Theme: Body Image. Director: Sheila Murphy, Producers: Micheal Hendricks and Tamara Lynch, 11 min. 24 sec.

Beauty Begins Inside: The "P" Syndrome. Director: Sheila Murphy, Producers: T. Lynch, I. Marks, M. Hendricks. 1996, 17 min. 17 sec.

Beauty Begins Inside: What's Eating You? 13 min. 25 sec.

Desperate Measures: Eating Disorders in Athletes. Producer: Sport Medicine Council of Canada.

The Famine Within. Director and Producer: Katherine Gilday; Narrated By Rebecca Jenkins. The National Film Board of Canada (NFB), 118 min.

Mixed Messages; Portrayals of Women in the Media. A five-part multi-media workshop analyzing negative images of women in the media. Co-producers: Friday Street Productions Ltd.

Someone To Talk To – Peer Helping in High School. Director: Annie Ilkow; Producers: D. Haig, W. Koeng, J. Merritt. Savoury Productions with the NFB, 1996, 26 min. 56 sec.

Thin Dreams: Young People Talk About Their Obsession with Thinness. Director: Susie Mah; Producers: Micheline Le Guillon and Gerry Rogers. The National Film Board of Canada, 20 min. 38 sec.

Widening the Circle: A Gathering with Young Women. Studio D, The National Film Board of Canada, 25 min 13 sec, 1992.

International Sources

Tessa: I Like Myself The Way I Am . . . How Do I Get Other People To? Writer/Director: Lori Larsens; Producer: Mial Cheylov, Booleg Films, 1991, 7 min.15 sec.

EDUCATIONAL PACKAGES

BC Centre of Excellence for Women's Health. *School Outreach Training Manual*, cost $20.00 available from BCEDA, tel. 250 383-2755, fax 250 383-5518, email www.bceda@islandnet.com .

Campbell, Denise and Bindu Dhaliwal (eds.) 1997. *Challenge the Assumptions*. Toronto: The Students Commission.

Challenge the Assumptions! is a multimedia educational package designed (by youth) to prepare youth to explore issues faced by young women in Canada and around the world. It includes a book, CD ROM, video, workshops and an Internet component. A wide variety of issues are explored, such as, body image, racism, labeling, classism, privilege, sexual violence, Western superiority, ableism, sexual exploitation, women in non-traditional fields and the distancing of young women from feminism.

Join Us: Become a member of CRIAW

The Canadian Research Institute for the Advancement of Women (CRIAW) is a national, not-for-profit organization committed to advancing the equality of women through research and publications about the diversity of women's experience. CRIAW bridges the gap between the community and academe, between research and action, through its partnerships and activities. Our members include independent researchers, students, academics, policy-makers, journalists, community activists, women's centres, universities, and others.

YEARLY MEMBERSHIP

- ❏ $ 15.00 Students, low income & women's centres
- ❏ $ 30.00 Regular
- ❏ $ 50.00 Supporting (includes a $25 tax receipt for your donation)
- ❏ $150.00 Sustaining (includes a one-year standing order for CRIAW publications and a $100.00 tax receipt)
- ❏ $100.00 Institutional (e.g. Women's Studies Departments, Advisory Councils)
- ❏ Educational Institutional Membership: designed for Universities, Colleges, and School Boards. Check to receive information on fees and benefits.

ADDITIONAL WAYS TO SUPPORT OUR WORK

- ❏ Make a designated, tax-creditable donation of $50, $100, $500, $1000 or any other amount to: CRIAW's Endowment Fund, which helps us become self-sustaining; CRIAW's research grants; or to be used for what is currently needed most.
- ❏ Check here for information about bequests - making a contribution to CRIAW in your will, or setting up a grant or scholarship in your name or in honour of someone else.
- ❏ Check here if you wish your donation to be anonymous, otherwise you will be recognized in our next national newsletter.

❏ Endowment Fund $ _____ ❏ Research Grants $ _____ ❏ CRIAW's discretion $ _____

❏ I enclose a cheque ❏ Visa ❏ Mastercard

Expiry date: _____ Signature: _____

Make cheque or money order c/o CRIAW/ICREF

Name: _____

Address: _____

Tel. (Bus): _____ (Res): _____

To Contact us or find out more:
Visit CRIAW's web site at www3.sympatico.ca/criaw
Contact the national office at 408-151 Slater Street, Ottawa, Ontario, K1P 5H3, Canada.
Tel: 1-613-563-0681. Fax: 1-613-563-0682
TDD: 1-613-563-1921 E-mail criaw@sympatico.ca

Check off information you would like to receive:
- ❏ publications catalogue
- ❏ author's guidelines and deadlines for submissions of manuscripts
- ❏ research grant application
- ❏ application for the databank of researchers
- ❏ application for scholarship in women's history

RECENT DOCUMENTS PUBLISHED BY CRIAW

Research Tools:
Women's Studies Practica: Students Linking Academe and Community. A Resource Guide. October 1999. Price: $10

Feminist Voices

VF No. 7 - La recherche sur les lesbiennes : Enjeux théoriques, méthodologiques et politiques sous la direction de Denise Veilleux. April, 1999. Prix: 10 $

FV No. 6 - Making New Feminisms: A Conversation Between a Feminist Mother and Daughter by Marilyn Porter and Fenella Porter. March 1999. Price: $10

VF No. 5 - D'une génération à l'autre : la transmission du rôle maternel au Manitoba français de 1916 à 1947 par Monique Hébert. August 1998. Prix :10 $

ORDER FORM

Please send me _____ copy(s) of_____ Price per title $ _____
Total $_____

Price includes postage/frais de poste inclus.

Name: _____

Address: _____

PLEASE MAIL THE ORDER FORM

❏ I enclose a cheque

❏ Charge my credit card   ❏ Visa   ❏ Mastercard

Number: _____

Expiry date: _____ Signature: _____

TO: CRIAW, 408-151 Slater St., Ottawa, Ontario, Canada K1P 5H3 Fax: (613) 563-0682